The Behavioral
Foundations
of Strategic
Management

THEORIES OF
STRATEGIC
MANAGEMENT

This exciting new series of sourcebooks in strategic management offers advanced students an intellectual grounding and foundation for their work in different specialist fields within strategy. Books in the series will be the sources researchers cite on theory in a given area, and will be the place we send our colleagues to begin to understand new work in a given area.

Each book in the series takes an area of substantial importance in strategic management research and sets out to clarify and integrate the theory related to the area. The series provides a stimulating forum for debate which will help move forward some of the central concepts and ideas in our field. By keeping the books as relatively brief overviews, the series also offers a useful map of ideas to a wider audience of students.

The Behavioral Foundations of Strategic Management
   Philip Bromiley

E-Business Models
   Thomas Brush

Entrepreneurial Process: From Foundation to Growth
   Harry Sapienza

Philip
Bromiley

The Behavioral
Foundations
of Strategic
Management

Blackwell
Publishing

BLACKWELL PUBLISHING
350 Main Street, Malden, MA 02148-5020, USA
108 Cowley Road, Oxford OX4 1JF, UK
550 Swanston Street, Carlton, Victoria 3053, Australia

The right of Philip Bromiley to be identified as the Author of this Work has been asserted in accordance with the UK Copyright, Designs, and Patents Act 1988.

First published 2005 by Blackwell Publishing Ltd

Library of Congress Cataloging-in-Publication Data

Bromiley, Philip, 1952–
    The behavioral foundations of strategic management / Philip Bromiley.
       p.   cm. — (Theories of strategic management)
    Includes bibliographical references and index.
ISBN 1-4051-2471-7 (hardcover : alk. paper) — ISBN 1-4051-2470-9
(pbk. : alk. paper)   1. Strategic planning.   I. Title. II. Series.

HD30.28.B765 2005
658.4′012—dc22

                                                                2004007689

A catalogue record for this title is available from the British Library.

Set in 10/12^{1}/$_{2}$pt Photina
by Graphicraft Limited, Hong Kong
Printed and bound in the United Kingdom
by MPG Books, Bodmin Cornwall

The publisher's policy is to use permanent paper from mills that operate a sustainable forestry policy, and which has been manufactured from pulp processed using acid-free and elementary chlorine-free practices. Furthermore, the publisher ensures that the text paper and cover board used have met acceptable environmental accreditation standards.

For further information on
Blackwell Publishing, visit our website:
www.blackwellpublishing.com

Dedicated to my wonderful family
(in alphabetical and chronological order):

Helene, Mike, and Roxanne

Contents

Preface

This book argues that strategic management scholarship needs a behavioral foundation. I hope to show that assumptions of rationality and equilibrium are inconsistent with rigorous strategy research, and that behavioral assumptions offer a sound and intellectually consistent foundation for strategic management scholars.

While I claim some novelty in offering these arguments in this form and addressed to this specific audience, I have an immense debt to prior scholars.

Much of this book restates the writings of Jim March, Dick Cyert, and Herb Simon. You may assume that any sensible sentences lacking a citation reflect something they wrote.

I have undoubtedly restated things other scholars have stated in recent years without giving due credit. For this inadvertent malfeasance, I ask your forgiveness. To keep the book short and to the point, I also have ignored many related literatures.

I have benefited immensely from colleagues and students in the Strategic Management and Organizations Department of the Carlson School, University of Minnesota. I could not ask for better friends and colleagues.

This book draws directly on prior joint work with colleagues Tom Brush and Lee Fleming, and with doctoral students Chris Papenhausen, Pat Borchert, and Sharon James-Wade.

Many of my friends and students have commented on earlier versions of this book. The students in my "Carnegie Class" at Minnesota offered comments. Students Jared Harris, Scott Johnson, Carla Pavone, and David Souder offered in-depth and insightful reviews. Likewise, Kent Miller (Purdue University) and Henrick Greve (Norwegian School of Management) commented on previous versions.

While these people have helped in many ways, I retain full responsibility for all remaining outrageous, inappropriate, and incorrect statements.

1 | Introduction

In recent years, strategy has developed an increasingly sophisticated theoretical and empirical research base. From a theoretical standpoint, several different approaches have been offered as a foundation for strategy scholarship, including industrial organization economics, resource-based view, and population ecology.

While these approaches have much to commend themselves, they have serious drawbacks, often because they make assumptions that contradict fundamental assumptions inherent in strategic management research. For example, models that assume managers make optimal decisions rule out the possibility of finding ways to improve managerial decisions. Alternatively, models that assume firms cannot change, as did some of the early work in population ecology, rule out studying how firm choices influence firm performance.

Most of what researchers actually assume and do about strategic management is most sensible in a bounded rationality or behavioral view of the firm. This book argues that strategic management should adopt a behavioral perspective. Although resting heavily on Cyert and March's (1963) behavioral theory of the firm (BTOF), I take a broader, although consistent, view of behavior. I try to provide researchers with a coherent framework and set of assumptions that fit the problems strategic management scholars address.

This introduction deals with several preparatory issues. First, it defines the objectives of strategic management research. We cannot evaluate differing approaches to strategy research without knowing its objectives. Second, it discusses what good strategy research means, and in particular what rigor means in strategic management research. Finally, it offers an initial discussion of the difficulties of conventional economic analysis in strategic management and the consequent need for behavioral assumptions. This discussion focuses on two core assumptions of traditional economic analysis – rational decision-making and equilibrium. Finally, I lay out a roadmap for the remainder of the book.

Objectives of Strategic Management Research

To discuss fundamental assumptions for strategic management research, we need to understand what strategic management research tries to do. I offer three objectives:[1]

1 *Explain firm behaviors at the strategic level.* The descriptive portion of strategy scholarship wants to explain firm behavior, while prescription must build on sensible models of firm behavior.[2] However, strategic management addresses firm behavior at a relatively aggregate level.
2 *Explain performance differences among firms.* We want to explain why some firms prosper and others do not. We consider firm environments, firm characteristics, and how firms use those characteristics.
3 *Provide suggestions to improve firm performance.* If we understand how firms behave and what influences firm performance, we open the possibility of offering suggestions for behaviors that improve performance.

This book argues that a behavioral view of corporate management provides the most sensible, logically coherent approach to these problems. By a behavioral view, I mean a view largely associated with the decision process view of the organization and a cognitive processing view of the individual, as opposed to an optimizing or economically rational view of the organization or individual. Most strategic management researchers implicitly take a behavioral perspective rather than taking the optimizing perspective to its logical conclusion.

Strategic management research attempts to address these three objectives scientifically. By scientifically, I mean that we require logically consistent theories and arguments, and that we submit these theories or arguments to empirical testing in ways that can be replicated. The logical consistency criterion makes science possible. Without a requirement for logical consistency, scientific discourse becomes meaningless. The arguments must have falsifiable empirical implications to answer the most fundamental empirical question: how would you know if you are wrong?

Philosophically, this book takes a critical realist perspective. That is, I assume firms exist, behavior exists and can be observed, beliefs exist, and things influence other things in a sensible manner.[3] I acknowledge the possibility of error in our scientific understandings. However, the questions posed above of explaining behavior and predicting performance differences and suggesting ways to improve performance make sense in a realist world, but may not make sense in some other frameworks.

What is an explanation?

Both objectives 1 and 2 use the term "explain." As scholars, we want to understand and explain how the items of interest behave. In a dynamic system, an explanation consists of a set of prior conditions, and a set of mechanisms or laws that operate on those prior conditions to generate predictions of new situations (Simon, 1992). Thus, we explain X by finding prior conditions A and B then applying a theory that relates A and B to X.

An explanation offers a mechanism by which the conditions interact to determine the outcomes of interest. Hedström and Swedberg (1998: 7–10) argue for mechanisms in sociological theory as follows:

> Assume that we have observed a systematic relationship between two entities, say I and O. In order to explain the relationship between them we search for a mechanism, M, which is such that on the occurrence of the cause or input, I, it generates the effect or outcome, O. The search for mechanism means that we are not satisfied with merely establishing systematic covariation between variables or events; a satisfactory explanation requires that we also be able to specify the social "cogs and wheels" (Elster 1989: 2) that have brought the relationship into existence . . . a mechanism can be seen as a systematic set of statements that provide a plausible account of how I and O are linked to one another . . . The approach advocated here does not rest with describing the strength and the form of a relationship between entities of interest but addresses a further and deeper problem: how (i.e., through what process) was the relationship brought about?

An explanation includes preconditions, mechanisms, and predictions. In a sound explanation, the preconditions should hold in the situation of interest. The mechanism should have some generality – a scholarship that allows idiosyncratic mechanisms for each event cannot build cumulative understanding. The predictions should be falsifiable. A Newtonian physicist wanting to explain the speed of a ball rolling down a ramp starts with certain facts (e.g., the height of the ramp, the angle of the ramp, etc.) and a set of mechanisms (e.g., Newton's laws). These together provide an explanation (and prediction) of the speed of the ball.

Many sciences use this form of explanation (Simon, 1992). Evolution and genetics explain the changes in a population based on laws and prior populations. Physical laws explain the position of the planets based on previous positions of the planets. This kind of explanation explains conditions at time t as a function of time t−1, etcetera, but does not necessarily have an answer for time 0. We can explain the rotation of the planets without explaining how they originally came into being. In strategy, this means all theorizing about firms does not have to originate with an explanation for the existence of firms.

An explanation depends equally on mechanisms and prior conditions. Thus, the correctness of the explanation depends equally on the correctness of both the preconditions and the mechanisms. A good empirical test of an explanation should test the mechanisms and prior conditions as directly as possible.

The correctness of the mechanism is critical to good explanation. Many now discredited theories predicted some outcomes quite well, but ancillary implications of the mechanisms did not hold up. A model assuming the sun and stars rotate around the earth predicts what most of us observe in the sky, but we reject this explanation because we now know the mechanism is incorrect.

Alternatively, the designers of sailing ships worked for centuries with an incorrect understanding of the mechanisms by which the wind moved the ship via the sails. They emphasized the positive pressure on the windward side of the sail as the primary mechanism by which the wind caused the motion of the boat. Later, researchers found that the negative air pressure on the leeward side of the sail actually provided most of the power (Curry, 1948; Harlé, 1961). The incorrect mechanism provided adequate rules – many built ships that worked well. However, given our current understanding of physics, a good explanation would consider both the low pressure on the lee side of the sail and the positive pressure on the windward side.

Radically different mechanisms can make similar aggregate predictions. For example, when it is hard to write good contracts, bringing certain transactions into a single organization instead of doing them through a market may improve efficiency. Two very different mechanisms might predict this improvement. First, internalization may make all parties identify with the organization or gain some inherent satisfaction from performance of the total organization, thus encouraging all to work toward overall performance. Second, and almost opposite, internalization may help control the parties who would otherwise lie and cheat; internalizing the transaction improves efficiency by improving controls. This dichotomy sounds a lot like the Theory X versus Theory Y discussion from the 1950s.

I discuss it later in regard to transactions cost economics. Clearly, these two mechanisms offer radically different explanations for the benefits of internalizing certain transactions. As scholars, we should care about the relative importance of each mechanism.

Understanding mechanisms has a particular importance if we want to generate prescriptions. While a strong statistical association may suffice for predictive purposes, if we want to manage something we have to believe in the causal mechanism. Just consider our internalizing transactions issue. Do we emphasize creating organizational identification or strong incentive and control systems? While a reduced-form, predictive device (e.g., internalization of transactions with characteristics X, Y, and Z improves efficiency) may satisfy for some uses, prescription demands understanding the actual mechanisms.

Rigor in Strategy Research

Rigor has been a concern for strategy scholars. Scholars from other disciplines have accused management researchers, and in particular strategic management researchers, of not being rigorous. In the early years of strategic management research, academics often debated the balance between rigor and relevance – Harvard Business School-oriented qualitative scholars saw their work as more relevant and those trained in traditional social science saw their work as more rigorous. While scholars trained in social science have largely taken control of the field, the underlying issue of rigor remains fundamental to our understanding of scholarship.

Strategic management research must meet conventional scholarly standards that I will refer to as rigor. Theory must be logically consistent and falsifiable with well-defined constructs and clear mechanisms by which constructs interact. Theory must tie clearly to empirical work (if the research does theory-driven empirical work). Measures and analyses must follow appropriate procedures. Without rigor, sensible scholarly debate becomes infeasible – we cannot debate if we allow logical inconsistencies, nor can we understand empirical results if we do not impose standards for such research. While scholarship can take many different forms, all forms need rigor.

Rigorous theoretical work takes a set of assumptions and logically derives implications. It clearly defines its assumptions and presents logical connections from those assumptions to its conclusions. Good rigorous theoretical work also recognizes or acknowledges implications of its logical development that may not be as desirable or likely to be true empirically as other implications. A logical argument implies all of its implications, not just those that its advocates find convenient.

Rigorous empirical work takes many different forms but all require consistency. For example, rigorous work developing grounded theory should explicitly identify the methodology used to collect and analyze the data to generate such grounded theory. Researchers must collect and analyze the data consistent with this methodology. The data analysis must lead directly to the theory generated. Alternatively, rigorous hypothesis-testing empirical work uses a coherent argument to develop the hypotheses. It uses valid, reliable measures of the constructs (which has implications for both the construction of the measures and the data-collection process), and analyzes the data using appropriate techniques to attempt to reject the hypotheses.[4]

Rigor constitutes a necessary but not sufficient condition for good scholarly research. One could do rigorous work that had no scholarly merit in a given academic tradition. A rigorous study of how dust accumulates in the offices of chief executives might interest someone, but does not contribute to strategic management.

Internal consistency and the ability to generalize relate to the rigor debate. Both reflect different applications of rigor. Internal consistency refers to the rigor within the theory and empirical study. The ability to generalize refers to whether the conditions of a study and another setting conform such that the study's findings can be logically applied to the other setting.

A study of decision-making by undergraduates at a major Midwestern university can be rigorous if the study is internally consistent and follows appropriate procedures. Its authors might have rigor problems if they generalize beyond that domain. Projecting results from a study of undergraduate behavior to top managers requires additional assumptions. If we found those assumptions untenable, we would reject generalizing from the study to top management.

Some scholars implicitly assume that rigor means mathematical derivations of hypotheses.[5] Newell and Simon (1956: 69–70) distinguish three kinds of theories:

1 *Verbal theories.* – An example of the statement in such a theory is: "Consumption increases linearly with income, but less than proportionately."
2 *Mathematical theories.* – The approximately corresponding statement in the mathematical theory is: "$C = a + bY; a > 0, 0 < b < 1$."

3   *Analogies.* – The idea that the flows of goods and money in an economy are somehow analogical to liquid flows is an old one. There now exists a hydraulic mechanism, the Moniac . . . I can give . . . a verbal (or mathematical) theory of the Moniac, which is, in turn, a hydraulic theory of the economy.

Simon and Newell argue that a physical analogy, for example the mechanical hydraulic model reflecting the consumption model above, may constitute an equivalent theory. They also argue that computer simulations may serve as theoretical analogies.

Simon and Newell distinguish among these kinds of theories primarily by their ease of manipulation by humans which is a psychological feature. They argue that the primary advantage of mathematical theories over verbal theories is not a logical difference, but rather the psychological difference that humans can manipulate the mathematical theory more easily. Newell and Simon (1956: 73) conclude that the three approaches offer different advantages and that "the construction of good theory is such an arduous task at best that is foolish to tie our hands behind our backs by limiting the range of tools that we utilize."

Rigor in one portion of a study may come at the cost of lack of rigor in another portion. For example, a rigorous mathematical derivation of certain predictions is often coupled with a very questionable practice of ignoring inconvenient predictions of the model. Alternatively, if an analysis makes factual assumptions, a very unrigorous selection of assumptions based on convenience may underlay a rigorous subsequent analysis.[6] Alternatively, an internally rigorous experimental study may be coupled with an unrigorous claim that the results have implications for behavior in dramatically different situations. Alternatively, rigorous econometric analyses may follow weak data collection or theory development. Rigor in one area often cannot compensate for lack of rigor in another. For example, if your measures are incorrect or your theory misleading, sophisticated statistical analysis can do little.

The need for logical consistency as a component of rigorous research requires that scholars use consistent assumptions. This makes blending of theories hazardous – different theories often have inconsistent underlying assumptions. Ecumenical arguments that try to include multiple theories often attempt to join theories with contradictory assumptions. Such efforts cannot lead to coherent theory.

To summarize, rigor constitutes a necessary condition for good scholarly activity. However, rigor does not inherently imply an advantage to one form of theorizing or empirical activity over another, and rigor must be evaluated across the entire span of a study, not just a portion.

Rationality and Bounded Rationality

Much of this book deals with the difference between rationality and bounded rationality assumptions. Let me begin the discussion here.

I will use the term rationality to refer to economic theory's concept of rationality, which means optimal decision-making. This concept assumes individuals have clear preference (utility) functions defined over outcomes and choose the alternative that maximizes this preference function subject to whatever constraints are faced. When applying this model to firms, most scholars assume firms' preference functions are profits, the net present value of profits, or shareholder returns. Since much of the argument below applies equally to individual and firm-level analyses, I will refer to a decision-maker who might be either an individual or firm.

The simplest application of rationality comes when we assume certainty. In this case, the individual or firm knows the consequences of all alternative actions and simply picks the one with the highest value. This only requires that preferences (described by a utility function) can determine that every item is equal to, or more or less desirable than, every other item and that such assignments are consistent (i.e., if we prefer A to B and B to C, we prefer A to C).

Savage (1972) extends this model to allow alternatives with multiple possible consequences. Here, the decision-maker knows all the alternative actions, all the multiple potential consequences of the alternative actions, and the probabilities of each potential consequence contingent on selecting a given action. The decision-maker chooses the alternative with the highest expected value. This extension normally requires that preferences be expressed as cardinal measures, i.e., it is meaningful to say that something gives twice the utility that something else does.

Savage (1972) notes that this approach assumes we trace out all the consequences of every alternative, which he recognizes as frequently unreasonable. If I want to choose a restaurant for lunch, this means I need to consider every restaurant available (hundreds in a normal city within a short drive). For each restaurant, I need to select the optimal travel plan (since travel time figures into my utility), the distribution of expected satisfaction and costs across all the foods I might select in each restaurant, and the potential future consequences of such choices (e.g., meeting someone interesting, or indigestion).

Most economic research makes these assumptions. For example, in efficient market finance, traditional theories assume everyone knows all available data and that all possible information has been derived from the available data. The "no rules for riches" statement discussed extensively later comes from such an assumption that everyone knows everything and acts rationally.

Herbert Simon criticized these assumptions, pointing out that they assume people know things they do not and can calculate things they cannot. Thinking about the restaurant example, most city-dwellers cannot name all the restaurants in a 3- or 5-mile radius. Even if we took the time to look up the names, we would still need their menus and experience with their food to begin to identify the potential outcomes associated with each restaurant. Secondary effects (e.g., the likelihood of meeting someone interesting) are even more difficult to forecast.

Even given the necessary information, we often cannot analyze it within a reasonable time. If it takes a few seconds to consider each menu alternative at each restaurant, we quickly find ourselves spending hours picking a restaurant for lunch. For most interesting questions, people cannot begin to do the calculations rationality models assume.

Massive literatures rejecting portions of rationality models have developed. The most direct is the behavioral decision theory literature (see Kahneman, Slovic, and Tversky (1982) and Yates (1992) for introductions). Problems that have been empirically demonstrated include:

1   Individuals often express preferences that violate the axioms underlying Savage's expected utility theory. A particularly important violation is that individuals code potential outcomes relative to some reference point rather than the final outcome as in utility theory.
2   Individuals handle uncertainty differently than statistical theories recommend. They often have systematically biased expectations reflecting (among other things) heuristics such as:
    • *Conservatism* (starting with a prior value and adjusting insufficiently to new information);
    • *Availability* (judging frequency by recalling incidents, making categories with more memorable incidents seem more frequent than they were);
    • *Hindsight bias* (remembering events that have occurred as more likely than they were before the event);
    • *Insensitivity to sample size* (seeing small samples as more predictive than they are and ignoring sample size in deriving judgments of likelihood);

- *Insensitivity to predictability of things they are asked to predict* (giving excessive confidence in predictions);
- *Ignoring regression to the mean, etc.*

The list of empirically demonstrated biases continues to grow with additional scholarly study.

Many rational theories also assume people know things they simply do not know. For example, macroeconomic models often assume all economic actors have the same model of the economy as the economist making the model (Sargent, 1993) when we know that the immense majority of the population cannot define GDP, let alone understand modern macroeconomics.

In contrast, bounded rationality approaches start with what we know about human and organizational decision-making and build from there. The next chapter discusses bounded rationality in more depth, and a subsequent chapter considers several defenses of rationality assumptions.

Summary of the Argument

To theorize about strategic management, scholars need to make assumptions about how firms and individuals make decisions. Two primary alternatives are available. First, following orthodox economics, scholars can assume that firms and individuals make optimal decisions. This assumption often goes along with assuming that industries reach equilibria where no firm can independently act to improve its position. Second, following the behavioral tradition, scholars can assume firms and individuals have bounded rationality. While they often act in ways intended to reach their goals, they generally do not have the information and cannot do the calculations necessary to select the optimal way to reach their goals. With such bounded rationality, firms and individuals often rely on norms and routines (see chapter 2).

The primary reason for preferring the behavioral approach is quite simple: it fits the facts while the optimizing approach does not. Research demonstrates that individuals cannot select optimal strategies in problems of even modest size (relative to strategic management problems). Behavioral decision theory has documented a multiplicity of ways people deviate from optimizing behavior. Research also demonstrates that organizations and individuals use routines to make decisions rather than making optimal choices.

Bounded rationality underlies the way we run the world. For example, many intellectual games are only interesting due to bounded rationality.

Chess has challenged great minds for centuries. However, in the rational analysis of game theory, chess is trivial – a two-person, zero-sum, perfect information game. One simply writes out the moves of all possible games and picks a move that guarantees a win. That no one could ever do this is irrelevant in most of game theory. Chess is challenging because people have bounded rationality. Consider the difference between tic-tac-toe and Go – the additional size of Go exceeds our ability to solve the game and so transforms a trivial game into a first-class intellectual challenge. Likewise, the additional moves available in chess make it more intellectually challenging than checkers.

In strategy, all our problems are immensely more complex than chess – we have hundreds if not thousands of potential moves coupled with great uncertainty about the state of the world and even the rules. In short, if we know people cannot select optimal strategies in the trivial world of chess, we can be sure they cannot do so in the immensely more complex world of business strategy.

That bounded rationality fits the facts about human decision-making better than rationality is an insufficient argument for many advocates of rationality, so I will examine additional problems that equilibrium and rationality assumptions create for strategic management scholarship. If we assume firms make optimal decisions, then we cannot explain performance differences among firms based on the quality of decisions the firms make – all performance differences must either reflect prior tangible conditions or luck. Likewise, if we assume firms make optimal choices then we cannot even imagine suggesting ways to improve strategic management. Finally, if industries are in equilibrium, then by definition management cannot improve their situations without collusion among firms. These clearly invalidate some of the objectives I identified for strategic management scholarship.[7]

Economically oriented scholars have attempted to cope with these problems but their solutions involve ad hoc assumptions of bounded rationality. Agency theory assumes the agent has perfect rationality, but the principal cannot tell how hard the agent is working. The resource-based view (RBV) assumes firms optimally use their resources, but also assumes managers cannot understand their resources or how to create them. If we need bounded rationality assumptions, we should make them consistently, based on empirical findings, rather than the convenience of the theorist.

Instead of an optimizing view of firms, most scholars in strategic management implicitly adopt a behavioral view. They assume firms can make better or worse decisions and then try to understand the characteristics of better or worse decisions. For example, in studying acquisitions, this means

assuming that appropriately matching features of the acquiring and acquired firms results in more satisfactory acquisition outcomes and that
some firms do this better than others (Hitt, Ireland, and Harrison, 2001). It
also suggests examination of inter-firm differences in the decision processes
and behavioral factors leading to acquisitions, and of the way acquisitions
are implemented and integrated (Jemison and Sitkin, 1986).

The remainder of this book develops these arguments. I hope it will serve
two purposes. First, for those who are implicitly behavioral, the argument
provides a coherent foundation for their research. Second, for those who
prefer optimizing and equilibrium models, the argument offers a challenge
to demonstrate intellectual rigor – that the problems being attacked can
be legitimately addressed while consistently assuming optimal decision-
making and equilibrium.

Outline of the Book

The remaining chapters of this book present a behavioral position and contrast it to other positions in the literature. Chapter 2 provides the basics
of a behavioral approach to strategic management. Chapter 3 considers
the economic assumptions of rationality and equilibrium and the problems
they create. Chapter 4 considers how a behavioral approach relates to a
number of conventional approaches to strategic management research.
Chapter 5 considers methodological issues, and the final chapter offers some
concluding remarks.

Before moving on, let me note three things this book does not do. First,
in arguing that strategic management needs a behavioral foundation, I
outline one of the major approaches to behavioral work. I am *not* arguing
that all research should resemble any particular flavor of behavioral work,
and so this book does not offer a comprehensive review of current research
in any area of behavioral research. Such a review is not essential to the
argument being made here.

Second, while I recognize numerous other relevant behavioral traditions
exist, I do not attempt to review them. Having a behavioral foundation lets
scholars import from these related traditions generally without inconsistency. Interested readers should go to better sources to learn about these
traditions.

Finally, this book does not present a "theory of strategy" from a behavioral
perspective. I am arguing that a behavioral perspective offers the best
foundation from which scholarship in strategy can build. The edifice is
under construction.

Notes

1 A colleague asked why the list does not include explaining the existence of firms and firm boundaries. I omit them for two reasons. If firm boundaries influence firm performance, then understanding differences in performance implies understanding firm boundaries. Furthermore, explaining the existence of firms is easy if we assume bounded rationality. The existence of firms stands more as a constraint on theorizing than an interesting problem; a theory that predicts firms should not exist is clearly deficient. Explaining the existence of firms to understand strategy is like explaining the existence of fish to understand marine biology. A theory that says fish should not exist is silly, or a theory that says they should look drastically different from what we observe can be rejected, but if we really want to understand fish, we do not spend our time worrying about why they exist.

2 This is directly analogous to medicine needing to understand how the body works as a basis for thinking about prescription. When medicine relied on an incorrect understanding of anatomy and physiology, prescription was often grossly misguided.

3 In seeing beliefs as real, a realist can comfortably deal with the influence of beliefs on behavior. Likewise, processes and power can be studied from a realist position. Some scholars might claim that recognizing the influence of perception moves one from the realist camp. Perhaps the distinction is that a realist can comfortably see politics, language, self-interest, etc. all influencing organizations (and other things), but, unlike some postmodernists or constructionists, still see organizations (and other things) as more than simply "what people agree on." The form an airplane takes is strongly influenced by social structures and beliefs, but the construction is still real. Do not try to fly in a socially constructed airplane.

4 While uncommon in the strategy community, rigorous exploratory research is quite feasible. Here one would be explicit about procedures for selection of variables and analyses. The procedures should be justified by the empirical problem being examined and should reflect the standards of scholars who concern themselves with exploratory data-analysis techniques (see, for instance, Hartwig, 1979).

5 The many philosophers who have written highly rigorous non-mathematical arguments provide exemplars of rigorous non-mathematical argument.

6 If the scholar only uses the analysis as a formal exercise, then the correctness of the assumptions may be immaterial. However, if the scholar implicitly or explicitly claims the analysis reflects some real behaviors, then the correctness of the assumptions becomes material. All strategy research claims some relation real behaviors.

7 As an intellectual basis to prescribe for practitioners, these assumptions create a quagmire. If firms are rational (make optimal decisions), no prescription can improve their performance. Managerial action demands a belief that the firm can improve its position.

2 | Basics of a Behavioral Approach

Any research involves simplification. Just describing something involves gross simplification from the infinite complexity of the real world down to whatever line of text or form of description one uses. As Simon notes (1979a), this level of simplification is inherently a satisficing process where the scholar decides how much simplification is good enough. Oddly, even scholars who build optimization models satisfice in their choices of assumptions and complexity (Simon, 1979a).

A behavioral perspective on strategy requires that the simplifications made reflect our understanding of individuals and organizations. Any given simplification emphasizes some aspects of individuals rather than others. Thus, one study might examine the influence of educational background on cognition whereas another might examine personality traits. However, both of these relate back to clear psychological foundations. The assumptions come from our understanding of the system (how individuals process information and make decisions) rather than from an ad hoc assumption chosen to facilitate mathematical analysis. As Simon (1997b: 26) notes in the context of economics, "I am not pleading here for a particular theory of rationality; I am pleading here for an economics that seeks out the facts of how people do react to situations and tries to base economic theories on those facts rather than on speculations made in an armchair."

While this book emphasizes bounded rationality, using this approach stands as a conscious simplification. People are more complex than our current bounded rationality models. Alternative studies may find it useful to modify this assumption to examine things such as the roles of emotion, organizational identification, norms, values, etc. in strategic decision-making. As with any scientific study, we simplify from our knowledge of reality to develop manageable theory and models.

Assuming bounded rationality leads to an information-processing view of the organization. Organizations process information, make decisions, and implement decisions. This emphasizes what information people have, how they process it, and what they do. March and Simon (1958) provide a detailed development of the organizational analysis from assumptions about individuals.

This chapter draws almost completely on prior research by Richard Cyert, James March, and Herbert Simon – it summarizes some of their work. Instead of littering this chapter with repeated citations to the same work, note that most of it draws directly from March and Simon's (1958) *Organizations* and Cyert and March's (1963) *A Behavioral Theory of the Firm*, both of which rely heavily on Simon's *Administrative Behavior* (1947; 4th edn: Simon 1997a). March's (1994) *Primer on Decision-Making* offers an insightful summation of the literature on decision-making. Scholars who wish to develop a substantial understanding of this literature should examine the entire set of major books.[1]

Basic Views of Decisions

As March (1994) notes, decisions are made using two basic approaches. First, most decisions come from people following rules of one sort or another. As March and Simon (1958: 141–2) say:

> Situations in which a relatively simple stimulus sets off an elaborate program of activity without any apparent interval of search, problem-solving, or choice are not rare. They account for a very large part of the behavior of all persons, and for almost all the behavior of persons in relatively routine positions. Most behavior, and particularly most behavior in organizations, is governed by performance programs . . . We will regard a set of activities as routinized, then to the degree that choice has been simplified by the development of a fixed response to defined stimuli . . .

For large organizations to function, most of their activities must be routine.

Second, some choices come from individuals or organizations searching for solutions to a problem. Such decisions, referred to as unprogrammed or problem-solving decisions (March and Simon, 1958), attempt to resolve a difference between what is aspired to or wanted (referred to as an aspiration level) and what is actually happening or expected to happen. The decision process involves searching for a solution that meets the aspiration level.

The remainder of this chapter introduces the primary concepts of the bounded rationality approach to organizations. As always, let me caution the reader to refer back to the primary works rather than relying overly on my efforts.

The following sections deal with:

- Bounded rationality.
- Routines
- Aspirations and search
- Slack
- Selection arguments

The bounded rationality approach to organizations is important but does not constitute all that has been done or known in behavioral work. I emphasize bounded rationality here because it is the approach I know best, and other scholars have used it to address the issues I want to address. Many other psychological and organizational theories offer important insights. These other theories are largely consistent with the bounded rationality view and so constitute a consistent approach.

Bounded Rationality

To understand firm behavior, we need a model of decision-making. Since people make most decisions in firms, we need to understand human decision-making to understand firm behavior. The model described here is bounded rationality.

This corresponds to a general proposition that to understand the behavior of a system at a given level, we need a simple understanding of the next lower level. To understand how firms interact in markets, we need a simple model of firm behavior. We can do a lot at a given level of aggregation such as market competition with a simple model of the lower level (firm behavior) if we use a correct model. However, these models of behavior below the level of primary interest must come from simplification of sophisticated understandings rather than scholarly convenience.

Some historical background may help understand the term "bounded rationality." Neoclassical economics assume individuals (and organizations) behave "rationally." By rationally, they mean actors choose the best of all possible alternatives – they have a consistent set of preferences and choose the optimal alternative given those preferences. These choices are unconstrained by information-processing – they do not choose the best of the alternatives they know about, or the best they can analyze, but rather choose the best of all possible alternatives. In this book, when I use the term "rational," I mean economics' global optimization perspective of decision-making.

Bounded rationality takes a less extreme position on choice. Bounded rationality means the actual ability of individuals to process information and make decisions. Such ability can be readily estimated in many important contexts.

This idea of bounded rationality has a long history in economics, although it has been discarded in recent decades. As Adam Smith talked about economic choice, he assumed that people had reasons for their actions. As Simon (1997b: 7) says, "the rationality of *The Wealth of Nations* is the rationality of everyday common sense. It follows from the idea that people have reasons for what they do. It does not depend on an elaborate calculus of utility or assume any consistency in what factors are taken into consideration in moving from one choice situation to another." As Simon (1997b: 8) says,

> What psychology has learned about the processes of human choice is consistent with the view expressed by Adam Smith. People do have reasons for what they do, but these reasons depend very much on how people frame or represent the situations in which they find themselves, and on the information they have or obtain about the variables that they take into account. Their rationality is a procedural rationality: there is no claim that they grasp the environment accurately or comprehensively. To predict their behavior in specific instances, we must know what they are attending to and what information they have.

Bounded rationality ties directly to research in cognitive psychology, which deals with the process by which people think and make decisions. The cognitive revolution has had sweeping implications across a variety of areas in psychology, other social sciences, and biological sciences. The cognitive approach views individuals as information processors.

We know a lot about how individuals process information. People have very large long-term data storage capability (long-term memory) but quite limited operating memory (short-term memory). People have strong pattern recognition capabilities but process almost all information serially. Even simple tasks like recognizing an old friend take 0.5 seconds (Simon, 1997b). Solving complex problems can take a long time. Conscious thinking works largely on the information in short-term memory. Depending on how you estimate it, short-term memory holds around five "chunks" of information at a time (Miller, 1956; Simon, 1974). While long-term memory has extremely large capacity, transferring from long-term to short-term memory takes time.

The limit on short-term memory and the length of time it takes to process information make it impossible for people to solve complex analytical or mathematical problems in the way economic theories assume they do. Few of us can multiply two three-digit numbers in our heads, let alone calculate an expected utility or any of the more complex things that appear in economic models.[2]

These micro-processes of information-processing lead directly to limitations on decision-making. For example, behavioral decision theory has examined ways that human decision-making systematically differs from optimal or economically rational decision-making. People suffer from many biases or systematic patterns that result in them making sub-optimal decisions, particularly in tasks involving uncertainty. Research demonstrates that people are poor intuitive statisticians. These problems are particularly important in strategy since almost all interesting strategy problems involve substantial amounts of uncertainty or even ambiguity.

Bounded rationality implies that we should limit our models of the individual or the organization by what we know they can and cannot do. This differs radically from the way bounded rationality has been adapted in economics.[3]

This bounded rationality or cognitive view of individuals leads to an information-processing view of organizations. Thus, the information people collect, store, transmit, and analyze is closely related to the decisions they make. Most organizational behavior follows routines or standard operating procedures (March and Simon, 1958). Even individual behavior largely follows routines: if I observed most of the readers of this book getting out of bed in their normal settings for two or three mornings, I could predict most of what they would do in a normal morning.

Probably the major first-order implication of bounded rationality is that people cannot analytically solve complex problems and so rely on simple rules. Problems that require handling large amounts of information mentally at the same time quickly become quite difficult.

Consider for example tic-tac-toe. Most adults find the three-by-three version of tic-tac-toe trivial. We solve this problem not by systematic analysis of sequential hypothetical move sequences, but rather by developing heuristics that guide our play. The game is uninteresting because we have heuristics that guarantee a tie or win.

However, if we change the game from three-by-three to ten-by-ten, it becomes quite challenging. Suddenly, the level of complexity challenges our ability to process information and makes the game interesting.

Older readers may remember when arithmetic textbooks for elementary education included sections on how to calculate quickly (see, for instance, Sticker, 1945). They taught the student how to multiply or divide two-digit or more numbers in the student's head. Most of us have difficulty handling such problems because we cannot retain the intermediate results in memory. Mental arithmetic tricks essentially reduced or avoided holding such intermediate results.

Robin Dawes (1971, 1979, 1994, 2001) examines this problem from a somewhat different perspective. He finds that three variable linear models can model many expert judgments. When we have experts looking at a complex set of data (graduate school applications for instance), we can build regression models of the individuals' decisions. The models generally need only three variables to predict these decisions. Such models have been developed and tested in a variety of contexts, including graduate school admissions (Dawes, 1971, 1979) and risk assessment in commercial lending (McNamara and Bromiley, 1997). Surprisingly, the model of an expert's decision-making often predicts better than the expert's actual judgment! Experts may have the right model, but they deviate from it (and err) when they make exceptions.

All of this comes down to arguing that a lot of human judgment, including judgment by experts, reflects relatively simple relations. Standard patterns of analysis, heuristics, and routines in organizations underlie and strongly influence human behavior.

A second feature of this process is that people generally search for solutions that are "good enough" rather than the best conceivable solution – a process that Simon referred to as *satisficing*. A high school senior searching for a college to attend has some idea of what he or she wants and searches until finding a few schools that fit. A computer programmer works until the program functions adequately. Usually, the individual does not know and could never know how good the best possible solution is. Furthermore, the individual seldom knows the likelihood that additional search will find better solutions. A scholar writing a paper works until the paper seems good enough. Most of us know that a better paper could be written on a given subject and that we might be able to write a better paper on the subject with additional effort. However, once we think the paper is good enough, we send it off.

The cognitive demands of satisficing are substantially below those of optimizing. As Simon has said, it is the difference between finding a needle in a haystack that is sharp enough to sew with, and finding the sharpest needle in the haystack. In fact, for all but the most trivial problems optimizing is simply infeasible: satisficing or some variant on satisficing may be the only feasible solution process.

In addition, people (and organizations) make decisions based on their beliefs and their implicit models of the world. These beliefs and implicit models can differ from reality. We all have such beliefs about what makes

a good marriage, how a business school should succeed, differences between races or groups of people, what women or men want, what drives
employee productivity, etc. We seldom question our implicit models, and
frequently we do not have the data to test our models even if we wanted
to do so.

Even when trying hard to make the "right" decision, people base their
decisions on their implicit models and beliefs and these may be incorrect.
In making decisions, people cannot act on some true state of the world if
they do not know what that state is.

While individuals must base their decisions on beliefs, the reaction of
the world depends on facts, or even the beliefs of others. A soft drinks company may believe Americans want a sweeter cola and may act on that
belief. The outcome will depend on Americans' beliefs about that cola (e.g.,
a belief that the old cola was best) and their actual tastes which influence
their purchases. I may believe the speed limit is 65 but be informed of my
error by a state trooper giving me a ticket for doing 65 in a 55 zone. I may
believe a given rope is strong enough to lift an object – the real strength
of the rope and weight of the object will determine how it comes out.
If I believe that my singing will make my colleagues happy, I may sing.
However, my colleagues' reactions depend on how well I actually sing,
not on my perceptions.

This differs radically from rational models. In rational models, the individual always chooses the option that offers the most utility to the individual. The individual operates with a correct model of the environment.
The individual does not operate on automatic pilot but rather continually
knows all the possible options and selects the best at all times. While some
models include search costs, most models assume the individual does not
have to search but rather chooses from all the available options. This is
reflected, for example, in the finance literature by its emphasis on criteria
for choosing capital investments and its complete omission of attention to
developing possible investments.

Any discussion must be consistent in its usage of rationality assumptions. Assuming bounded rationality in some areas and rationality in
others makes little sense. Williamson (1985) makes a similar point when
he says that we should only compare realistic institutional arrangements
rather than comparing a particular institutional arrangement to some
idealized perfect world. Likewise, comparing the efficiency of an optimizing
solution to a bounded rationality solution is like imagining a race between
a racecar and bicycle. Asking which is faster is silly, but asking which suits
a given purpose may make sense (and checking whether you really have
a racecar is essential).

Some economists argue that bounded rationality is simply optimization taking into consideration information processing costs (e.g., Conlisk, 1996). As Williamson (1985: 46) says, "[i]t is sometimes argued that bounded rationality is merely a convoluted way of stating that information in costly." In other words, people act as if they are boundedly rational because they optimally balance the costs of searching further against expected gains.

This argument says people derive optimal solutions to (1) how much effort to put into solving the tangible problem, and (2) the tangible problem conditional on the decision on effort to expend. This requires far more information-processing ability than simply optimally solving the tangible problem. Arrow (1986) notes that economic theory attributes increasing computational power to individuals to accommodate these extensions. Conlisk (1996) notes that it creates a problem of infinite regress as the individual must calculate the optimal amount of search to put into solving the tangible problem, the optimal amount of search to put into solving the optimal amount of search problem for the tangible problem, and so forth. Yet the initial reason for bounded rationality was the recognition that people lack the information-processing power assumed in optimizing models.

The simplest response to the "bounded rationality is optimizing" argument is simply that it does not conform to the facts. When people use routines to solve a problem, they seldom think about the information-processing costs that lead them to do so. They just do it.

Coming back to Simon's example of searching for a needle in a haystack,

- Traditional economics assumes you find the sharpest needle;
- Behaviorists assume you search until you find a needle sharp enough to sew (or you give up); and
- Believers in "bounded rationality is optimizing" assume you search until the expected returns to additional search (i.e., the expected value of having a sharper needle) are less than the expected cost of additional search.

These are three very different models. They require different amounts of information and calculation or search. They predict different outcomes. Baumol (2004) and Arrow (2004) make similar points. As Arrow (2004: 52) stated, "a boundedly rational solution cannot be described as the optimal solution to an optimization problem in which computational delays or costs are included in the formulation of the problem." The bounded-rationality-is-optimizing argument is just an attempt to claim that everything remains optimizing. Bounded rationality and optimal behavior considering search costs differ.

Routines

Given bounded rationality, March and Simon (1958) discuss how organizations function. If individuals were truly unboundedly rational (i.e., perfect optimizers), organizations could be described by their constraints and objectives. Instead, with bounded rationality, organizations function by (1) subdividing complex problems so that individuals can address smaller, more manageable problems, and (2) making many activities routine. Marketing employees do not worry about production, production staff do not worry about marketing, and top management does not learn the details of either one. All rely on an enormous amount of standardized behavior that lets them get on with their activities.

Complex organizations could not function without routines. Think of all the things that must happen so that a faculty member meets a set of students on the first day of class. We need routines that recruit and select students for the university. We need routines that help students find places to stay, advise students on courses, and monitor their progress. We need routines that provide buildings, maintenance, heating, lights, and the plethora of other things that property management requires. We need other routines that recruit all the employees involved, pay them, provide health benefits, etc. We need routines to get textbooks that match the courses offered and that make sure that students and an appropriate faculty member appear in the classroom at the same time. All of these activities must mesh consistently so that the great majority of the time students appear in the right classroom with the right professor.

Businesses also require routines. From recruiting, to training, to building maintenance, to payroll, to ordering products and materials, to production, sales, and distribution, a business's everyday operation reflects a mass of interrelated routines. Routines dictate the immense majority of what happens in a business.

Routines serve several purposes in organizations. First, they allow coordination and increase reliability. Consider the things necessary to get a faculty member and class together. If intelligent people were assigned each of these tasks without routines, their interrelated actions would certainly not mesh properly. The simple task of having students meet a professor in a classroom becomes very difficult without routines. Think about getting up in the morning in a family. Most families have routines that try to avoid everyone needing the bathroom at once, that make sure appropriate people get to school or work at appropriate times, etc. Even in a family, utines differ radically across areas. For example, lawyers look to s and rules to solve problems. Accountants track processes and onsistency between differing figures. Empiricists collect data while develop models. In our MBA classes, students with marketing unds often recommend tactics to increase sales while those with on or accounting backgrounds want to reduce costs.

ach routines. A book on how to play chess includes many heuris- outines such as "control the center of the board" or "put a rook in file." Likewise, when teaching someone to diagnose problems with ing or home repairs, we give them routines that tell them where to rst and how to interpret what they see.

ile routines play central roles in the operation of organizations, they strongly influence strategic decision-making. The data available, the problems become identified and labeled, how alternative actions ome identified, and the set of feasible actions all depend on the organ- ion's routines. Much of what we teach deals with these routines. For mple, we teach how to design accounting and information systems. We ch rules for making decisions and running operations.

Routines can be conscious or unconscious. We all have many routines e are unaware of – habits of speech, action, etc. We also have routines e understand well – the route we take to work, etc. Part of the power f routines in organizations derives from their taken-for-granted position. They channel information and attention in particular ways, guide feas- ible actions, structure thinking, etc., sometimes in ways managers do not appreciate.

Researchers must avoid misinterpreting the behavior of routines as con- scious strategic choices. A routine response may differ greatly from what the top management might have chosen if it had examined the problem. For example, how we treat customers and staff comes mostly from opera- tional routines rather than a conscious decision by top management about how a particular customer or staff member should be treated. Employees sometimes apologize for treating customers poorly by saying they had to follow the rules.

Routine behavior also comes from norms of appropriate behavior (March, 1994). We do many things because they are appropriate. I help junior faculty because I believe senior faculty should do so. Given satisfactory service, I leave tips at restaurants, even if I do not plan to return. Such things flow from a rule of appropriateness – much of the service and assist- ance faculty provide to their departments and schools cannot be justified as in the individual faculty member's self interest. We do it because it is appropriate.

a very small organization, these r(
coordination and efficient functionir.

Businesses face the same coordinat
people make sales, filing the right forr.
being shipped, bills sent, etc. Producti(
obtain appropriate materials and that s;
right manner. All depend on building mai.
information-processing, etc., following th\
able services. Formal procedures manuals ;
these routines, and informal or undocumen.

Routines subdivide attention. They subdiv
viduals to deal with manageable parts of it inst.
The sales staff assigned to a given product wo\
that directs their attention to selling that pro(
development, production, and shipping of that p\
ing the corporation's other sales issues. This econ
information-processing. Within academe, disciplii
break the world down so that individuals can have s\
areas of interest. A business scholar who felt compelle
latest in several business disciplines would find it prac
get anything done and is unlikely to come out with a (
of any particular area.

Routines economize on cognition. Routines mean th
not reanalyze how to clean the building every night. Lik(
vidual in the system does not have to sit down and think
little action. Part of the setup costs in a starting a new j(
learning how the routines operate to get things done. On(
about routines like computer programs: while I can sit down ;
certain things in a standard programming language (for exam.
write a regression routine in Basic), it is massively more efficier.
likely to have errors) if I use packages that have been designed
my problem directly. Organizations are built from packages k\
routines.

While I have emphasized routines in organizational functionin;
also play a role in expert judgment. My HMO has routines that
the physician diagnose my problems. The nurse takes my pulse and t
pressure and writes down my symptoms for the physician. For m\
problems, the physician also has routines. If you go in with a cold, y
can expect the physician will look down your throat, check in your ear
thump your back, and so forth.

These r(
precedent
look for c
theorists.
backgro
product
We t
tics or
an op(
plumk
look f
W
also
way
bec(
iza
ex
te

Having routines or rules of appropriateness does not make decisions trivial. We may not know which rules or appropriateness criteria to evoke. The archetype of this problem is a moral dilemma where two different rules apply to the same event and give radically different implications. Furthermore, rules can be hard to apply; well-specified procedures can be hard to execute.

Finally, routines change. Often, routines modify routines. TQM procedures help companies change their other procedures. Schools have procedures to change the curriculum, and curriculum change alters other routines. Process engineers routinely search for better routines or processes and their outputs modify routines. Some corporations have routines to search for acquisition targets and routines to integrate newly acquired companies. Firms that often introduce new products will have routines for developing and introducing new products. Part of organizational learning comes from incremental changes in the parameters or functioning of ongoing routines.

Top management can change routines, but changing routines is hard. Routines interact in complex ways, so changing routines requires substantial understanding, sophistication, and continued effort. The Harvard Business School's General Electric cases illustrate the importance of routines. Many GE innovations came as new routines and routines that modified other routines (e.g., the planning system, portfolio analysis, and TQM). The strategic planning system is a routine that focused attention on high-level problems, and then provided inputs for other routines (such as budgeting). Portfolio analysis tools routinely structured the analysis, both indicating and justifying certain changes (acquisitions, divestitures, and funding). TQM is explicitly a set of routines that change other routines.

Routines manage simple adaptation. In corporations, budget routines target unprofitable products for elimination. Hurdle rates in capital budgeting routines guide investment toward high-return activities. Marketing researchers routinely assess customer needs to guide product development. In universities, routines target classes and departments that draw few students. Normally, rules change other rules in ways that continue the basic direction of the organization.

When routines modify other routines, they generally make changes within predefined areas and have built-in repertoires of possible modifications that strongly influence their impacts. Historically, cost-cutting routines tried to reduce waste, labor, and other costs within the current plant and product line. Such routines seldom considered outsourcing or re-engineering the product to reduce production costs. Such routines did not search for modifications to add customer value. Such routines seldom looked across stages in the value chain. Other routines that modify routines evidence similar patterns.

Aspirations and Search

Having discussed routine decisions, we now turn to non-routine or unprogrammed decision-making based on satisficing. March (1994) notes that routines and satisficing reflect two radically different ways to make choices. They both derive theoretically from bounded rationality. Without bounded rationality, neither makes much sense. The satisficing model assumes decisions come from looking for alternatives that exceed a criterion or aspiration level, whereas the routines model sees decision-makers judging things by their category and applying the appropriate rules.

When do individuals or firms engage in non-routine decision-making? Most of the time, most organizations follow routines. Individuals and firms search when their expectations or current performance fall below their aspirations. Failing to meet aspirations defines a problem. Non-routine decision processes attempt to solve these problems. The aspiration argument applies equally to individuals and organizations so I will discuss both. Aspiration-level effects in organizations come partially from individuals adopting organizational aspirations, but also from formally stated aspirations or targets.

Aspiration levels

Individuals and organizations aspire to certain levels of accomplishment in various dimensions. An aspiration level constitutes a target – people feel they have succeeded when they exceed, and that they have failed when below, the aspiration level. As an individual, I have numerous aspirations, including those relating to my salary, my publication record, and my weight. Corporations often publicly state aspiration levels for sales and profits. Capital market analysts forecast firm performance and criticize firms that do not meet the forecasts. Within corporations, divisions also have aspiration levels. Firm budgeting and management systems set dozens if not hundreds of targets for divisions on things including cost per unit, backlog, quality, and so forth. A student may aspire to a specific grade.

Aspirations have two important features – dimension and level. Dimension means the things regarding which we aspire – salary, publications, sales, profits, etc. For each of these dimensions, we have a level, which defines when the dimension is satisfactory.

The dimensions of aspirations can reflect numerous factors. The reward system clearly influences aspiration dimensions. If the reward system emphasizes units sold, individuals will aspire to sell certain numbers of units. The membership and relative power of the members of the top management team may influence dimensions of aspirations. In a firm dominated by marketing, I would expect more sales and market aspirations, and in one dominated by finance more financial and capital market aspirations. Social factors also influence the dimensions of aspirations. For example, norms on social responsibility create aspiration levels for corporate charitable giving and minority hiring.

Levels for aspirations come mainly from two comparisons – with one's own past performance and with the performance of similar others. Firms compare their current performance to their past performance. A firm that has grown at 15 percent a year worries if it only grows at 5 percent, whereas a firm that has been unable to grow is elated at 5 percent growth. Budget processes that display last year's figures in the first column and planned figures in the next encourage such comparisons. A student who has mainly received Bs and so aspires to Bs will feel elated over As and depressed over Cs.

Early theoretical work modeled aspirations as a function of previous aspirations and the difference between aspirations and performance. This resulted in aspirations being an exponentially weighted moving average of multiple prior performance levels. However, most empirical studies have used single-year comparisons. Which better matches managerial aspirations is an empirical issue. The issue need not have a general solution – aspirations in one area may adapt more quickly than those in another.

A firm or individual also compares performance to others that are considered similar. In a low-profit industry, a relatively high-profit firm may feel very comfortable with a performance level that would be considered desperately bad in a high-profit industry. Likewise, in high-growth industries managers may aspire to 50 or 60 percent growth a year whereas in many low-growth industries or declining industries they rejoice at 5 percent. Many firms use direct measures of relative accomplishment such as market share. If a student's friends got As in a class, the student may aspire to an A there.

Social comparison depends on availability of data on comparable firms and individuals – the available information defines the feasible comparisons. For example, companies collect and publicize data on quality in new automobiles. This encourages car companies to focus on initial quality rather than long-term quality. In some organizations, employees know everyone's salary, while in others salaries are kept secret. The first facilitates inter-personal comparisons.

Generally, aspiration levels rise more quickly than they fall. People quickly accustom themselves to high pay levels. If circumstances change, they regret lower pay levels for a long time. A firm that has been dominant will continue to aspire to dominance long after it has become less powerful, while a firm that reaches dominance almost immediately aspires to continue it.

In both comparisons, aspirations have a positive bias. Firms aspire to slightly higher performance than their past performance. Individuals aspire to higher income or higher grade points than their current income or grade points. Both firms and individuals aspire to being above average. This positive bias keeps individuals and organizations from becoming totally stable and satisfied in the long run.

Two additional reference points become important for firms with very low performance. Making or losing money stands out as an obvious important distinction. Bankruptcy also has a strong place in the aspiration metric. Even if all firms in an industry lose money, we would expect none of those firms to be satisfied losing money. Likewise, even if all one's competitors face bankruptcy, bankruptcy remains an undesirable outcome for most firms.

A firm's behavior depends on which reference point becomes the primary focus of attention. A firm that expects to survive but is close to bankruptcy (i.e., is just above that reference point) may behave in a similar manner to a firm that aspires to the industry average performance and is just above it.

Aspiration levels function as hurdles and reference points. Being over versus under an aspiration level matters.[4] Firms and individuals also may define their performance relative to these aspiration levels. For example, in the stock market, meeting the analysts' earnings forecasts matters – being above or below the forecast is important. The distance above or below the forecast also matters. The aspiration or forecast stands as a reference point from which the decision-maker defines relative performance.

Firms have aspirations along multiple dimensions (e.g., sales, profits, quality), and corporate responses vary depending on which aspiration dimension is not met. The aspiration model defines a multiple hurdle problem (i.e., exceeding the aspiration level for each dimension) rather than a unitary goal to be sought or a function to be maximized.

Individuals and organizations compare their performance or their expected performance to these aspiration models. Depending on the context, the firm might use expectations or might use actual performance. For example, in the formal planning process, top management may demand divisions raise their forecasts to generate plans that meet top management's aspiration levels (Bromiley, 1986). These plans become aspiration levels (targets) for the managers involved (often backed up by rewards and punishments). In the operating cycle, firms routinely compare actual outcomes to budgets (aspirations) and then take action if the outcome is below budget.

Search

Failure to meet the aspiration level results in a search for changes to raise performance above the aspiration level. The aspiration level violated strongly influences the search.

Failing to meet an aspiration level generates a problem – a difference between expectations (or current situation) and aspirations on a specific dimension. Thus, failure to meet quality goals defines the problem as a production problem involving quality. Sales below the target defines a sales problem. The specific aspiration level violated defines the problem.

Individuals and organizations search for solutions near the problem before searching further away. A lack of sales triggers search in the sales area before searching in product development, quality, or customer service. Managers may blame a quality problem on production workers because they are "closer" to the quality problem than factors such as the overall production process or product design.

Firms have systematic patterns in their search processes. Facing a problem, a cost-oriented firm like Knight's Emerson Electric searches for cost reduction opportunities. Innovation-oriented firms like 3M try to innovate their way out of trouble. Such orientations influence the firm's search for solutions.

Search may end in two ways – by finding a satisfactory option or by lowering aspirations to make an option satisfactory.

Organizations search for alternatives that meet their aspiration levels and accept the first that does so, a process called satisficing. This satisficing process implies that the sequence of search for potential solutions matters. Searching in a given area first strongly increases the probability that the solution will come from that area. Potentially better solutions that might have been found later go undiscovered. Organizations seldom fully develop more than one solution.

This single-solution process is so common that organizations have routines that try to combat it. Government agencies often require multiple bids for purchases. In production, the Taguchi method (Roy, 2001) calls for experiments that vary production parameters and consider a continuum of quality outcomes instead of our traditional approach of searching until finding a solution that matches an arbitrary quality level. Strategic planning systems ask managers to examine overall positions rather than focusing on specific problems.

If the organization cannot find a solution that meets the aspiration level, it lowers the aspiration level. Thus, the student who was always the brightest in class in college will try even harder when finding himself or herself an average student in a doctoral program. If still not excelling, the student may become accustomed to being an average doctoral student. If a firm accustomed to 20 percent growth cannot find ways to maintain that rate, it will lower its aspiration level for growth. The firm may decide that 10 percent growth suffices.

Alternative variations

The literature acknowledges two other conditions under which non-routine search may occur. If the firm exceeds its aspiration level substantially, it may search. Alternatively, solutions may search for problems.

Organizations that have exceptionally high performance, i.e. that have performance sufficiently far above their aspiration levels that they are confident they will exceed their aspirations, may experiment knowing they are in no danger of missing aspiration levels. Such firms can afford to play knowing that they will be okay.

The process of organizations searching for solutions may be reversed; sometimes solutions search for problems. Management may want an airplane or a new building so it searches for reasons to buy them (i.e., management looks for problems the desired solutions could solve). An external innovation promising high returns also constitutes a solution which searches for problems. A company may not recognize a problem until someone selling a solution convinces management that they have the problem. In academe, a desirable candidate may lead a department to request a new position: the existence of the candidate (the solution) results in the department generating problems to justify adopting the solution. This logic has reached its most extreme statement in the garbage can model (Cohen, March, and Olson, 1972; March and Olsen, 1979) where choice situations become defined by which solutions, problems, and participants attach to them.

Slack

Organizations have slack. When times are good, slack builds up. Firms store slack in financial instruments, excess staffing, excess pay, etc. Slack provides the ability to deal with setbacks. Faced with lowered sales, new regulations, new competitors, etc., firms call on slack to reduce costs, fund projects, staff initiatives, etc.

Just as individuals have some desirable level of fat, organizations can have too little or too much slack. Slack serves a positive function. As firms reduced their slack in recent years, some managers found they had no staff to deal with studies or unanticipated problems: everyone was overloaded doing their normal jobs. Slack helps buffer the firm from the winds of the environment. However, maintaining slack costs money so too much slack can lower profitability.

While in some areas firms consciously manage slack (for example, most firms set policies for working capital levels), slack usually develops without such conscious analysis. In good times, firms are less careful about restricting hiring so divisions hire excess staff. In good times, firms may pay off some of their debts or buy back some of their equity. Managers may allow themselves additional perquisites and may allow additional benefits to workers. All of these constitute forms of slack that can be brought down or used when times turn bad.

The Ecological or Selection Argument

Bounded rationality models predict specific sub-optimal behaviors by firms. Empirical results often support these predictions. Economically oriented listeners frequently ask, "Why don't the good firms simply drive these bad firms out of business?" Given how often I have heard this question, it merits comment.

This is a selection question – why don't selection processes result in the survival of only the optimally fit?

Selection processes work at the corporate or at least division level. Corporations survive or fail, not individual routines or corporate activities, just as individuals or organisms in biology survive or fail as whole organisms, not specific parts of the organism. This partly explains the substantial diversity in both animal and organizational populations. A particular person, animal, or organization may do some things well and others poorly. Overall, it may survive. If a corporation does 10,000 different things, it may do some very well, some very badly, and most passably and come out as an average firm. Selection at the firm level does not neatly select the best routines.

The firm-level selection argument also generally assumes that *perfectly managed firms exist and can supplant poorly managed firms.* Bounded rationality implies firms never do anything optimally (except for a few technical things which may be optimized within very narrow bands). No optimal firms lurk in the bushes to attack sub-optimal firms.

In addition, selection only works on the population that exists at any given time, and selection takes time. At best, selection can pick the best of the current firms for survival. It cannot generate a perfect firm if none exists. It also takes time for the more fit in the population to replace the less fit.

Consider the US automobile industry in the 1960s and 1970s. The Big Three US automakers survived profitably for many years. The entry of the Japanese competitors demonstrated that none of the Big Three operated even at the "best in class" level, let alone optimally. The Japanese demonstrated the Big Three were inefficient, produced low-quality products, and did not produce some products customers clearly wanted. Since, before the entry of the Japanese companies, the Big Three dominated the market and none of the Big Three produced efficiently, with high quality, or the smaller cars customers wanted, selection forces did not work. After Japanese competitors entered the industry, the selection process changed.

That selection results in survival of only the most efficient firms is termed historical efficiency (March and Olsen, 1989) and examined directly by Carroll and Harrison (1993, 1994). Carroll and Harrison (1994) simulate industry dynamics using coefficients from empirical studies of organizational population dynamics. They simulate an industry where less efficient incumbent firms face entry by more efficient rivals. While the more efficient entrants often eventually dominate, in many simulation runs the less efficient incumbents maintain dominance over the more efficient entrants. This is surprising because Carroll and Harrison (1994) simulate 500 years of competition. Heightening the level of competitive interaction increases the probability that incumbents dominate. As Carroll and Harrison (1994: 747) conclude,

> our findings suggest that matter-of-fact use of this assumption [that more efficient firms dominate] might lead to incorrect inferences about competition as much as one-third of the time in real-world settings when complete competitive histories are used. The error rate is likely to be higher for censored data.

That is, Carroll and Harrison conclude that, 500 simulated years after entry (using meaningful parameters for selection rates), less efficient incumbents continue to dominate more efficient entrants one-third of the time. Since entrants come to dominate later than incumbents, observing the industry earlier increases the chance of less efficient incumbents dominating the more efficient entrants. In many of their trials, entrants took hundreds of years to dominate an industry. We should not assume the forms of the dominant firms today are the most efficient of the currently available forms.

Environmental heterogeneity can also deter the domination of the efficient. Consider restaurants. Different customers want different things – low prices, good food, good service, location, particular kinds of food, etc. Even those who want good food or service may differ in their evaluations. This heterogeneity allows the survival of a heterogeneous population of firms which cater to different customer groups. To assume the observed firms are the most efficient of available forms requires assuming efficient entrants into each of the plethora of sub-markets, restrained competition that lets them grow, and sufficient time for them to dominate (Carroll and Harrison, 1994).

Populations change through two general mechanisms: selection and adaptation. Selection is noisy – the level of selection is high enough that substantial variation can exist in surviving firms. Selection only operates within the existing population. Selection often takes a long time to alter the existing population. In addition, selection may depend on differing factors at differing times. In one era of an industry's life-cycle, selection may be on innovation, but later it may be on production efficiency. A firm that would have been king later may not survive long enough to be crowned.

Adaptation also matters. The Big Three improved quality and offered smaller cars after the Japanese demonstrated customers wanted them (and took a substantial portion of the market). US automakers did not go bankrupt (although Chrysler was close) to be replaced by new firms, but rather changed. Could adaptation result in optimal firms?

Adaptation or learning has problems. While adaptation of routines and search allow firms to learn, they may not learn. March and Olsen (1988) present a very nice discussion of problems in learning. Figure 2.1 lays out the model.

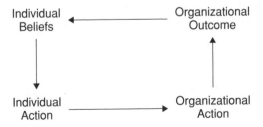

Figure 2.1 The complete cycle of choice
Source: March and Olsen, 1988: 338.

To learn, we need a process where (1) what we do influences what the organization does, (2) what the organization does influences the observed organizational outcomes, (3) organizational outcomes influence our perceptions, and (4) our perceptions influence what we do. Any of these four connections can break down:

- What we do may not strongly influence what the organization does. Despite individual action, routines may dominate behavior. The organizational change literature speaks to the difficulties of getting decisions implemented. Even what the CEO orders does not necessarily happen. A lower-level manager may take appropriate action but not change the organization's actions.
- What the organization does may not influence its outcomes. While a firm changes some things, its competitors, customers, suppliers, and general environment also change. Competitors, customers, suppliers, and the environment may influence firm success more than the firm's actions.
- The outcomes may not strongly (or appropriately) influence our beliefs. Given noisy environments and noisy outcomes, we often do not know how to adapt our beliefs to the outcomes. We have too few observations to tease out the relative contributions of a dozen factors that influence performance. Managers routinely credit failed projects to bad implementation and success to good decisions. Managers may believe things that are not true (termed superstitious learning). How rapidly we should update our beliefs given new data is problematic: if we adapt too rapidly we may adapt to many short-term blips, but if we adapt too slowly we may miss real changes in the environment.
- Our beliefs influence our behavior. Behavior (or decisions) can reflect routines. Our beliefs might suggest one thing, but we do another out of loyalty, sense of duty, or simply habit. Alternatively, our beliefs about one thing may not be evoked when a related problem comes up. We might not see Choice X as an example of Problem Type Y, and so not apply our understandings of such problems to Choice X. This problem is quite familiar to college instructors who find students unable to apply material taught in earlier courses to later courses.

In short, selection works somewhat and firms learn somewhat but neither process guarantees we reach any particular outcomes. Specifically, they do not guarantee optimal firm behavior. You do not have to run very fast to win the race if all your competition is very slow. Relative to an ideal optimal firm, all real firms are slow.

This fits my experiences in day-to-day life. Many mediocre businesses survive – I have eaten at many mediocre restaurants, bought poorly designed and made merchandise, and had poor service in stores. Not that mediocrity is the norm (although it may be in some areas), but rather selection pressures and adaptation only work slowly if at all. Efforts to adapt (e.g., the e-business craze) can result in maladaptive changes, which damage performance. Many "well-managed" firms lost money by ill-advised moves into e-business.

Finally, even well-directed adaptation does not guarantee the firm achieves a good or optimal fit with its environment. Consider an organism adapting to its environment. How well it is adapted at any given time depends on the speed with which it adapts, and the speed with which the environment changes. If the environment changes as fast as or faster than the organism, the organism may never become well adapted to the environment.

In business, some things adapt quickly (e.g., prices for retail gasoline) but other things adapt very slowly (e.g., industry structures in banking, financial services, or airlines). Although deregulation began in the 1970s, the structure of the financial services industries continues to change drastically. Likewise, the airline industry has failed to achieve a structure where most firms break even (a necessary constraint for any long-run adaptation). If the factors influencing the appropriate industry structure change more quickly than the industry's structure, the industry may never have the appropriate structure for its environment. Similar problems can exist in other areas (i.e., not just industry structure) where the firm's environment changes quickly.

Even in a stable environment, adaptation may not lead to optimal forms if the terrain over which the organism adapts is not smooth – the firm may adapt to a local situation, reaching a local maximum rather than the global maximum (see Levinthal, 1997, 1999). This happens, for example, in competency traps where an organization gets so good at Technology X that it cannot move to the better Technology Y (see, for instance, Lynn, 1982).

Instead of the populations of optimally fit firms assumed by economic researchers, I see populations of firms with varying capabilities. Depending on the challenges of the day, such varying capabilities translate into varying fitness levels. The observed populations are not optimal.

The "optimal drives out non-optimal" argument was popular in finance theory. For decades, financial economists argued that models of capital markets only needed to deal with optimal investors since either (1) the non-optimal would go broke, or (2) the optimal would take advantage of the non-optimal and drive the market to optimal positions (often by arbitrage). Recent work in finance clearly demonstrates that these arguments are flawed. For rational investors to take advantage of non-optimal investors the optimal investors must know who the non-optimal investors are and when they are investing – neither of which is feasible in general (Summers, 1986). If the rational cannot eliminate others in the simple world of capital markets, why would they do so in the more complex worlds of strategic management?

Neither selection nor adaptation reliably guarantees that a population of firms behaves optimally. While both may improve average performance, the two processes have sufficient problems and noise that heterogeneous populations of firms should constitute the norm. This fits the facts.

Two Criticisms of the Bounded Rationality View

While many scholars use the bounded rationality approach, several criticisms have been leveled at it. This section addresses two of them.

One of my Harvard Business School (HBS)-trained colleagues worried that the information-processing view omitted managerial imagination and creativity. Part of this comes from the difference between an HBS view and the conventional empirical view of scholarship. Managers certainly make what we call innovative decisions. If we use the terms imagination and creativity to connote surprising or unanticipated decisions, then almost by definition such decisions cannot be systematically explained or predicted. We can acknowledge they happen, but may be unable to predict or explain them.

An information-processing view does suggest when activities we call creative should occur and the probable direction of such activities. Creativity is more likely on occasions when the firm undertakes search. The direction creativity takes should reflect a variety of behavioral factors – the definition of the problem, prior managerial experiences, information systems, etc. Cognitive psychology work on creativity also offers a basis for studying managerial creativity.

The information-processing view also has been attacked as offering a sterile view of individuals – omitting values and emotions – and ignoring important societal values. Argyris (1973, 1976) says that, by its emphasis on explanation and prediction, it helps managers exploit others rather than improving the situation of the employee.

Although March (1994) demonstrates that the approach allows for a variety of motivations and March (1996) partially addresses the creation of values, the criticism is partially correct – to focus on routines and bounded problem-solving, bounded rationality approaches use a simplified model of the individual that ignores several factors, including emotions. It has a rudimentary model of motivation, but lacks the sophistication of schools of study primarily concerned with motivation. Whether such simplifications seriously damage explanation is an empirical problem that merits empirical examination. If they do, the bounded rationality model would require extension to include such factors.

The second criticism, that it emphasizes explanation rather than taking an explicitly value-driven position, reflects a clear difference in assumptions about researcher values. Scholars in this tradition have generally taken a positivist stance and tried to explain and understand behavior, rather than taking a normative stance of evaluating behavior against some predetermined standard. While Argyris calls this position mini-Machiavellian, it clearly matches the norm in many areas of scholarship. Much of strategic management does take a normative position, but one opposed to Argyris's position – we often assume increasing firm profits is desirable.

Summary

This chapter has outlined a fundamental model of the organization. The organization operates on standard operating procedures that both maintain and slightly adapt the organization. When aspirations exceed current performance or expected performance, the firm searches for ways to improve performance to meet aspirations. The aspiration-expectation process acts to allocate attention and consequent search (see Ocasio, 1997). Such search starts by looking for small modifications but can lead to larger changes if the small ones do not suffice. The firm accepts "good enough" solutions rather than continuing search for the most desirable outcome. Slack buffers all of this.

Firms based on this model can interact in markets. Instead of optimally choosing prices and outputs, behavioral models predict adaptation by sequential feedback. Such feedback means firms react sensibly to most things. If wage rates increase, production costs may exceed aspiration levels (and total expenditures for wages exceed management's aspirations for wages). Subsequent search starts in production and looks for ways to make production costs acceptable. Replacement of labor with capital may result. In models where the world is simple, stable, and follows nice functional forms, adaptation may eventually result in outcomes that resemble the predictions of optimizing theories. However, as discussed above, this is generally not true. The world is complex, not fully stable, and does not follow nice functional forms so firms seldom reach such optimal values. In this model, firms behave sensibly, but not optimally.

In particular, most firms aspire to profits. Since aspirations rise above past performance, firms will seek ways to increase profits. Thus, behavioral models accommodate a logic of sensible behavior – if firms know something would increase profits, for the most part, they will do it.

This comes with two strong cautions. First, it differs from optimal decision-making in that optimal decision-making says firms immediately optimize performance, not that they tend toward higher performance. Second, it sees this tendency toward increased performance as part of a complex process where a variety of other factors influence the firm.

Given my background, I over-emphasize the decision-making approach. However, this behavioral approach is consistent with the numerous lines of research in organizations theory and social psychology that can inform our research. For example, institutional theory and population ecology emphasize the stability of organizations and institutions based on routines (Scott, 2001). Likewise, behavioral decision theory is consistent with an information-processing view; an information-processing explanation should underlie the heuristics and biases of behavioral decision theory (Smith, Benson, and Curley, 1991; Curley and Benson, 1994). Most behavioral approaches to organizations are consistent with the approach presented here although offering different emphases and parametric assumptions. Thus, the bounded rationality approach can be extended to include such approaches without logical inconsistency.

Given this view of organizations, let us evaluate equilibrium and rationality assumptions.

Notes

1 I would see the basic readings including Simon's *Administrative Behavior*, March and Simon's *Organizations*, Cyert and March's *Behavioral Theory of the Firm*, and March's *Decisions and Organizations*, *The Pursuit of Organizational Intelligence*, and *A Primer on Decision-Making*.
2 Economists do not specifically claim that people calculate these things necessary to make optimal decisions. Rather, they say that people act as if they optimized. However, they offer no mechanisms by which people could act as if they optimized.

3 Economists generally assume that bounded rationality means decision-makers do not have perfect information but do have extensive information-processing power and complex understandings. This is discussed extensively in chapter 3.

4 This implies that decision-makers react very differently to positive or negative events. Many scholars have applied this to risk-taking and predicted that risky potentially negative events (threats) are treated very differently than risky potentially positive events (opportunities). A large number of experimental and archival studies support this prediction. It may even have a biological foundation. Using positron emission tomography, Smith, Dickhaut, McCabe, and Pardo (2002) find that different parts of the brain activate in response to threats than in response to opportunities.

3 | A Behavioral Critique of Rationality and Equilibrium[1]

The primary alternative to a behavioral perspective in strategy is an economic perspective. This economic perspective underlies much of the work in the resource-based view, as well as in industry analysis. I argue that such an economic basis is inconsistent with the problems and objectives of strategic management research.[2]

This discussion of economic views emphasizes models based on *economic rationality* and *equilibrium*. Economics includes a variety of kinds of work, but these two concepts underlie much of that work and almost all of the work that has been imported into strategic management research.

Rationality and equilibrium are central to economic theory. As Krugman (1996: 3) says, "the overwhelming thrust of conventional theory has been to say that agents are not only intelligent, they maximize – that is, they choose the best of all feasible alternatives. And when they interact, we assume that what they do is achieve an equilibrium, in which each individual is doing the best he can given what all the others are doing." That is, conventional economic analysis rests on two pillars: (1) *rational optimization* by agents – here rational optimization means that the agent chooses the best of all possible alternatives, and (2) *equilibrium* – here solutions are such that no actor can improve his or her situation by current actions (Nelson and Winter, 1982).

Throughout, I will use rational to mean optimal choice, and equilibrium to mean solutions are such that no actor can improve his or her situation by current independent actions (termed a Nash equilibrium). Both equilibrium and rational have other meanings, but in this book I will use them in this way unless specifically noted. This follows common usage in economics.

Rationality assumes actors optimally use all the data available to them in determining their choices. In some variants, actors consider the cost and problems of computation. In others, scholars assume rational expectations to avoid modeling how actors deduce information from the data available (Sargent, 1993).

The mix of economic and casual usages of "rational" has created an interesting rhetorical twist. Some economists refer to decisions that do not match optimal decision-making as "irrational" (see, for instance, Shleifer, 2000). Some also claim that irrational behavior is unpredictable. The rhetorical trick here is that not being rational in the economist's terms does not imply being irrational in conventional usage. Funk and Wagnalls (1963: 715) defines irrational as: "1. Not possessed of or incapable of exercising the power of reason. 2. Contrary to reason; absurd; senseless." One can do less than the economist's rational choice without being irrational according to conventional usage. Bounded rationality is not unreasoned, absurd, or senseless behavior.

This chapter begins by outlining the basic behavioral critique of rationality and equilibrium assumptions. It then addresses several of the conventional responses to these criticisms. Next, it considers several related issues on rationality and equilibrium in the context of strategic management.

The Behavioral Critique of Rationality

Behaviorists have criticized neoclassical economics for many years (see, for instance, Veblen, 1908). Sen (1977) notes that J. Butler's *Fifteen Sermons Preached at the Rolls Chapel*, published in London in 1726, objects to economists characterizing humans as completely self-interested. Their critiques rest heavily on the accusation that the conventional economic assumptions of rationality and equilibrium are incorrect. The critiques argue that economic models assume people behave in ways they do not and assume people make calculations they do not and cannot make. Particularly in the 1950s and 1960s, a debate occurred in the economics literature featuring Milton Friedman, Herbert Simon, Paul Samuelson, and others.[3]

Let us begin by clarifying what rationality means in economic analysis. As Nelson and Winter (1982) argue, rational models in economics have three components:

1 Actors have clear, consistent value functions, whether these are profits, shareholder returns, or individual utility;
2 Actors face a clear set of alternative actions and the outcomes of these actions are well defined at least up to an understood statistical distribution; and

3   Actors choose the alternative that maximizes expected value from the
    set of alternative actions.

Each component necessary for rational decision-making can be empirically rejected. Depending on order of presentation, manner of presentation, and other factors, individuals often make decisions that demonstrate
they do not have consistent value functions. Factors like reference levels,
anchoring, etc. clearly influence choices in ways they should not with
a consistent value function.[4] Often, actors do not know all the possible
actions and have little or no idea of the outcomes contingent on actions.[5]
Without consistent value functions and not knowing the outcomes of
all potential actions, actors cannot choose the action which results in the
optimal outcomes.

To a behaviorist, the assumption of optimal or rational behavior by firms
seems unreasonable.[6] As with individuals, firms cannot identify all their
possible actions, nor can they track all the implications of the actions and
assign probabilities to each one. By definition, a firm that makes optimal
decisions does not make errors; the idea of any entity not making mistakes
seems preposterous.[7] Likewise, by definition, optimal behavior implies
current behavior cannot be improved. The idea of a business that cannot
be improved is likewise peculiar. I doubt that many readers of this book
have worked in a business where he or she could think of nothing to improve. Yet, the rationality assumption assumes nothing can be improved
in any business.

Empirical results reject the rationality assumption. At the individual
level, the rational model translates into maximizing expected utility. The
immense behavioral decision theory literature soundly rejects expected
utility maximization.

Examining corporate decisions shows they often could not be maximizing profit – the decision process simply does not collect or analyze the right
data to make that kind of decision. For example, instead of equating marginal cost to price, firms use mark-up pricing rules. Baumol (2004) notes
that firms often do not know their marginal costs or even average costs at
the product level, and they have even less information on demand elastic-
ities – data that even the most elementary economic analysis assumes
every firm has automatically. That firms in trouble find substantial cost
reductions that they did not find when they were doing well supports the
non-optimizing position; optimizing firms run optimally efficiently all the
time. Furthermore, even the simplest interactions with businesses indicate
some are better run than others. In short, the data strongly demonstrate
that most firm and individual behavior is not optimal.[8]

A behaviorist would also not assume markets are in equilibrium. The conventional Nash definition of equilibrium, that no firm can independently improve its outcomes, ties into rationality that assumes every firm has taken the best actions to maximize outcomes. If firms have not acted optimally, then some firm should be able to improve its position and the market is not in equilibrium.

So, how have economists responded to the argument that firms and people cannot make optimal decisions? Most of the responses implicitly acknowledge that rationality assumptions are factually incorrect. Let us consider some arguments economists have used to justify using their assumptions.

Responses to the Critique

Rationality assumptions are untestable

Some have argued that the optimal decision assumption cannot be empirically refuted (Boland, 1981). As Viale (1997: 154–5) says,

> Once they [assumptions about rationality] have been introduced, are the principles which characterize the economic agent aprioristic and unfalsifiable, hence empirically uncontrollable, or are they, instead, falsifiable, controllable and in the final analysis, corrigible? The first is, of course the epistemological option that prevails in economics. It does not matter how assumptions are introduced – whether by observation, introspection or intuition or completely hypothetically – but once they have been, they are turned into aprioristically unfalsifiable truths . . .

Obviously, the general practice of making assumptions and claiming they are unfalsifiable truths is flawed. Many assumptions are empirically testable.

The mass of work in behavioral decision theory clearly refutes expected utility maximization as a universal rule for individual decision-making. A variety of experiments show how individuals violate basics of expected utility maximization (see Kahneman, 1994; Kahneman, Slovic, and Tversky, 1982; Yates, 1992). For example, utility maximization requires that the choice among alternatives depends on the final positions that come from those choices. Different wording of the alternatives (e.g., presenting them as gains or losses) can switch the preferences of decision-makers.

Evidence also demonstrates that firms operate in ways which cannot lead to optimal decisions. For example, firms often do not have the data and do not collect the data to analyze decisions rationally. They also use clearly inferior practices in many areas (e.g., inventory management, scheduling) when better methods are available. That operations research can increase firm profits by improving scheduling, inventory management, and so forth demonstrates that firms were not operating optimally.

Assumptions of rationality are indeed testable, and the evidence strongly rejects them.

Only optimizers survive – selection

Some have argued that we only need a model of optimizing firms because market competition and evolution eliminate all non-optimizers. By some unstated process, the adaptation will reach equilibrium, an argument Nelson and Winter (1982: 26) call "at best . . . an *ad hoc* mix of maximizing and adaptive models of behavior."

This is a variant of the selection argument discussed at length in the previous chapter. As Cyert and March (1992: 231–2) note,

> The argument is simple: competition for scarce resources results in differential survival of rules that produce decisions that are, in fact, optimal. Thus, it is argued, that we can assume that surviving rules (whatever their apparent character) are optimal. Although the argument has a certain charm to it, most close students of models of adaptation have suggested that neither strategic choice, nor learning, nor selection, will reliably guarantee a population of rules that is optimal at any arbitrary point in time.

Correctness of assumptions doesn't matter because optimization predicts well

Milton Friedman (1953) offers a very different argument for using obviously incorrect assumptions. He argues that the correctness of the assumptions is irrelevant if a model predicts behavior correctly at the level of interest to the researcher. In fact, Friedman (1953: 14) says,

> In so far as a theory can be said to have "assumptions" at all, and in so far as their "realism" can be judged independently of the validity of the predictions, the relation between the significance of a theory and the "realism" of its "assumptions" is almost the opposite of that suggested by the view under criticism. Truly important and significant hypotheses will be found to have "assumptions" that are wildly inaccurate descriptive representations, and in general, the more significant the theory, the more unrealistic the assumptions . . .

Friedman wants to explain aggregate behavior; he claims economics wants to explain the behavior of markets and higher levels of aggregation. He offers an example of explaining expert behavior in billiards using Newtonian mechanics. He argues that we do not have to worry about the rest of the problem – Newtonian mechanics, while certainly not what billiards players use to solve their problems, explains the behavior on the table.

Friedman's position has been described as positivist. As Caldwell (1984: 2–3) says, "If you ask a working economist what science is, and why what he is doing qualifies as scientific, his answer will be peppered with positivist buzz-words."

A large literature developed around Friedman's paper. Overall, philosophers of science agree that Friedman's simple positivism and instrumentalism fall short as a philosophical basis for scientific research (Caldwell, 1984). Musgrave (1981) calls Friedman's approach instrumentalist in that Friedman claims theories should not try to truly describe reality or to explain phenomena but rather simply predict some features. This differs greatly from my view of a theory or model. I assume we as scholars want to explain phenomena, and a good explanation implies belief in the mechanism of the theory, not just that it predicts well. Furthermore, any attempt at prescription requires a belief in the mechanisms of the theory.

While far better scholars than I have addressed these issues, let me offer some simple comments. For Friedman's argument to work, we must agree that (1) optimization predicts well, and (2) prediction alone is the crucial test of theories.

DOES OPTIMIZATION PREDICT WELL?

Some have argued that economics is justified in its methodology by its extensive history of factually correct predictions. For example, in a recent exchange in economic geography over profit rate versus profit maximization, the profit maximization advocate fell back on this claim (Barnes and Sheppard, 1992; Harwitz, 1998; Sheppard, Haining, and Plummer, 1998).

However, the core *optimization assumptions alone make almost no predictions* (Heiner, 1983). As Heiner (1983: 561) says,

> a long list of confirmed predictions would be persuasive evidence in favor of a theory. Yet, it is here that we have a problem. Suppose we really asked to see the list of clearly implied, unambiguous predictions that have been derived from our basic optimization models.
>
> The answer to this query, one that would be admitted by many practitioners in the field, is that at best we have developed a very short list. All sorts of behavior is consistent with or plausibly suggested by optimization

models, yet is still not predicted by them. For example, optimization models have never been able to imply the Law of Demand (buying less of a commodity when its price rises), which is probably the oldest and simplest behavioral regularity in economics . . . We could pursue a number of other examples, all of which suggest that conventional models have never really been fruitful in generating testable implications.

Heiner (1983: 561) reports a story that Armen Alchian told a graduate price-theory class that "the only clear implication of consumer theory is that with more income, a consumer will buy more of at least something." This implication comes from an accounting identity that assumes income will be spent, not from optimization.

How do we have all these apparently successful predictions when the underlying theory does not make such predictions?

Often, economic theorizing *starts with knowledge of the empirical relation that the theory is supposed to explain rather than predicting it.* Arrow (1986) notes that economists engage in a form of theoretical data-mining where they modify their models until they get solutions that fit the empirical data. Arrow (1986: S398) says, "Rationality also seems capable of leading to conclusions flatly contrary to observation." As Conlisk (1996: 685) says, "economic research often seems to work backwards from the empirical findings to whatever utility maximization will work. Where the empirical arrow falls, there we paint the utility bullseye."

Such theoretical data-mining is possible because *the predictions largely come from ad hoc ancillary assumptions, not from rationality.* A theoretical development uses both core theoretical constructs and a set of ancillary factual assertions (Simon, 1997a[1947]). For example, utility theory says nothing about the actual things that give an individual utility – it just says that people behave consistently (Sen, 1970, 1977). Almost all predictions from utility theory require ancillary assumptions. For example, agency theory generally assumes agents are risk-averse and do not get utility from the performance of their employing company. These empirical assumptions have no direct justification in utility theory. They often simply reflect the convenience of the scholars building the model. As Williamson (1985: 44) says, "[m]any economists treat behavioral assumptions as a matter of convenience." That is, the assumptions have neither theoretical nor empirical support. Scholars make such assumptions to move from utility theory to a model that predicts certain behaviors. However, as Arrow and Conlisk note, theorists usually start with the empirical regularity and then manipulate assumptions until the model fits it, so it is not surprising that the model fits the regularity.

Furthermore, given the ancillary assumptions one can readily generate the optimizer's predictions without assuming optimization – the predictions are not unique to optimization. Simon (1997b: 89) notes that:

> Nearly all of the conclusions reached by neoclassical theory that have the solidest empirical support (e.g., that demand curves slope negatively, supply curves positively, that excess demand drives prices up and excess supply drives them down) are reachable without the assumption that economic actors are maximizing or minimizing anything. Most of the conclusions that are drawn in the theory of public choice, or for application to various domains of "applied" economics do not rest on the assumptions of optimization, but do rest heavily on the *ad hoc* assumptions about the content of the utility function (e.g., that people mainly want wealth, or power) and about the ability or inability of people to form accurate expectations (e.g., the money illusion).

The ancillary assumptions give the power.[9] The explanatory power of economic models comes from rough approximations of the right environmental variables, not from the theoretical model of decisions used (Arrow, 1986; Conlisk, 1996; Goldberger, 1989; Simon, 1986). Arrow (1986: S385) says,

> rationality hypotheses are partial and frequently, if not always, supplemented by assumptions of a different character. . . . I have not carried out a scientific survey of the uses of the rationality hypothesis in particular applications. But I have read enough to be convinced that its apparent force only comes from the addition of supplementary hypotheses.

While most analyses involve numerous ancillary assumptions, let me briefly note an example most readers may be familiar with – the assumption of risk aversion. Utility theory does not require or imply risk aversion. The theory has no explanation for individuals being risk-seeking or risk-averse since, within utility theory, these are simply curvatures of utility functions.

Almost all agency theory predictions come from assuming that principals are risk-neutral and agents risk-averse. With risk-neutral agents, the problem of incentives for agents becomes trivial. With risk-seeking agents, it becomes another problem altogether. Assuming risk-seeking or risk-averse principals also transforms the problem. I know of no direct empirical evidence to support agency theory's risk preference assumptions.

In finance, models predicting that stocks risk and return correlate positively assume individual investors are risk-averse (Fama and Miller, 1972). Even if this made sense for individual investors, whether it makes sense now that professional investors and funds hold most investments is unclear. Given the benefits of having extremely high performance (i.e., investors move to funds with the highest historical performance), one could argue that funds have an incentive to take more risks in hopes of being near the top of the return rankings.

These agency and finance predictions come directly from ad hoc assumptions of risk preferences, but the two theories make opposite assumptions about the same people. Capital market theories assume risk-averse investors while agency theories assume the same investors (called principals) are risk-neutral. This seems odd to me. It demonstrates the arbitrariness of the assumptions and the problems inherent in refusing to empirically validate assumptions.

That the power of economic theories comes from ancillary assumptions has implications for testing. Scholars pick these ancillary assumptions so the predictions fit the empirical data.[10] If the predictions are not supported, the scholars reject the ad hoc assumptions, not optimization. This means they really test the ad hoc assumptions, not the theory. All scientific approaches that attempt falsification face this problem; testing the theory usually requires additional non-theoretical assumptions. However, the problem is magnified when (1) the assumptions are ad hoc, and (2) scholars do not test the assumptions or intermediate mechanisms of the theory.

We usually *test against a particular parameter equaling zero rather than alternative sensible models.* This use of zero for the null hypothesis is referred to as the extreme null hypothesis (Ijiri and Simon, 1977; Savage, 1972). Sometimes, it is obvious a firm should react to the factor so the null hypothesis of zero is not particularly interesting. Empirical work based on optimizing theories seldom tests whether firms optimize – rather, it tests against the hypothesis that the firm does not react at all to the factor.

What if two plausible theories predict the same sign for a parameter? Often optimizing and non-optimizing theories predict similar responses to external factors (see Nelson and Winter (1982) for several examples). Here, testing against a null hypothesis of zero does not help reject the alternative explanation. One can differentiate among such alternative models if they predict different parameter magnitudes. Alternatively, we can test ancillary predictions of the theories or predictions of the intermediate steps the theories assume (Bromiley, 1981). Conlisk (1996: 684–5) notes, "instead of testing the predicted effects of optimization against the predicted effects of competing theories, we tend to test against the nonsubstantive null hypothesis of no effect. This is somewhat like arm wrestling a rag doll; it doesn't prove anything – unless the rag doll wins."

Let me offer two examples. First, assume a conventional production function model of the firm (output a function of capital and labor with the firm minimizing the cost for a given output level) with instantaneous, costless adjustment. If the price of labor increases, a sensible reaction is to use less labor. However, an optimizing model predicts much more – it predicts the firm moves to the precise labor/capital ratio that minimizes production costs. Showing a negative relation between price and quantity of labor supports the sensible reaction, but does not test the optimization prediction. The immense majority of tests based on optimization models test for sensible reactions, not optimal ones.

The second example comes from the immense literature that estimates production functions (the relations between national capital, labor, and output). Simon (1979b) demonstrates that estimates of aggregate production functions do not differentiate between the hypothesized production function and an accounting identity between measured output, labor, and capital. National accounts formats often enforce the accounting identity among the three variables. Berndt (1976) actually constructed a measure of output from capital and labor data, and then used those data to estimate non-linear production functions relating capital and labor to output. Estimating non-linear production functions can give highly significant parameter estimates, but be misleading if the paper tests against the extreme null hypothesis instead of a sensible alternative model (the accounting relation).

Even so, many optimizing predictions do not hold. While finance assumes firms act to maximize shareholder wealth, the most carefully examined corporate action (mergers) shows just the opposite: firms purchasing other firms lower their own share prices. Alternatively, consider scale economies. To avoid a number of very undesirable predictions, micro-economics assumes increasing economies of scale followed by decreasing economies of scale at large scale. As Marris (1997: 140) says, "the theory that survives from Marshall in every elementary textbook of economics today, is the theory of that horrible curve that goes up and down like a toilet pipe for which in the long run there is no theoretical or empirical justification whatsoever. Nobody has yet produced any empirical evidence that there is any upper limit to the size over which a firm could be efficient." Marris (1997: 140) points out that we do not "find in any data a robust negative correlation between the sizes of firms and their profitability."

Finally, Friedman's argument assumes that *researchers can select the implications of the argument that they wish to test and ignore the others.*

Hutchison (1960) says that theoretical derivations of empirical hypotheses involve two kinds of statements. Pure theory statements represent logical relations among symbols manipulated within a theoretical structure. In pure theory, no inferences are drawn concerning the empirical world. Alternatively, applied theory uses the pure theory framework to make statements about the empirical world. In applied theory, Hutchinson argues that scholars make assumptions about what is empirically true. Whereas a pure theory of a market is simply an intellectual structure, an applied theory claims the analysis relates to the real world. Since Friedman and strategy research both claim relevance to the real world, we concern ourselves here with applied theory.

In applied theory, one makes factual statements about the world. An assumption that firms maximize profits stands as an empirical assertion that this is true. As Hutchinson (1960: 23–4) says,

> the statement made is that of a certain relation between the premise p and the conclusion q. "*Since* p *therefore* q" is equivalent to two propositions, (1) the proposition of pure theory "If p then q", and (2) the empirical synthetic proposition "p is true" (and, if one likes, thirdly, the further assertion as true of the empirical synthetic proposition q).

As Hutchinson demonstrates, the statement of applied theory involves specific propositions about the correctness of the assumptions (p) and the predictions (q). In evaluating the correctness of the statement "Since p therefore q", it is just as legitimate to consider whether the "empirical synthetic proposition 'p is true'" as it is to consider the truth of "the empirical synthetic proposition q." Any attempt to test an applied statement such as "Since p therefore q" must deal with both p and q. If we know p is not true, even if we find q true, we would not infer support for "Since p therefore q."

Consider a logical argument that assumes A and B to predict C and D. Any legitimate test of this argument must deal with A and B as well as the outcomes C and D. To assume A makes the assertion that "A is true" a condition of the argument. If we know A is not true, no finding concerning B, C, and D can tell us anything about the correctness of this argument. Indeed, if we know A is never true, then the logical statement can never be true. For example, consider the logical argument: (1) fish are rocks; (2) rocks do not breathe air; therefore (3) fish do not breathe air. To evaluate this, we must to consider all three portions of the argument. If any of the prior conditions is untrue, then no relation between the other prior condition and the outcome is informative about the argument. Finding many rocks that do not breathe air does not justify the logical argument. An applied theory's assumptions (like rationality) stand as testable predictions that are critical to assessing the correctness of the theory.

Furthermore, if the logic predicts more than one thing, then a good test of the logic addresses both. To test some predictions and not others allows an ad hoc selection of the hypotheses most likely to be upheld.

Optimizing models often make implausible predictions their supporters ignore. Of particular interest, Heiner (1983: 586) notes, "the observed regularities that economics has tried to explain on the basis of optimization would disappear if agents could actually maximize."

For example, rationality generally predicts relatively little capital market activity. In the traditional efficient market model of financial markets (incorporating rational expectations), stocks should trade relatively little. As Arrow (1986: S389) says, "in macroeconomic models involving durable assets, especially securities, the assumption of homogeneous agents implies that there will never be any trading, though there will be changes in prices. This dilemma is intrinsic." What do price changes mean without trading? Furthermore, efficient market models predict very little trading. If all traders know the market is efficient, they know they cannot make abnormal returns from trading and so should not trade. This prediction of little stock trading is just as legitimate a prediction of the theory as many others, but is clearly rejected by the data.[11]

In short, one cannot claim that a large and successful set of predictions support optimization. Most of the predictions come from models using ad hoc assumptions chosen to fit the data. Heiner (1983) argues that most such predictions would disappear if all actors were rational (see Findlay and Williams (1979, 1980) for similar arguments in finance). The tests seldom if ever differentiate among alternative models or test the optimization proposition per se. In addition, scholars often only test the implications of optimization models they anticipate will be supported, and ignore the others.

PREDICTION IS THE APPROPRIATE TEST OF A THEORY

Prediction is unsatisfactory as the true test of a theory. Just checking the predictive ability of models does not offer us evidence to support the underlying logical arguments of a model.

When several different logical arguments make the same prediction, that prediction cannot differentiate among the arguments. For example, slow adjustments in allocations of funds could be justified as maximization within a slowly changing world or incremental adaptation (Bromiley, 1981). Many of the predictions of rational actor models can come from simpler models. Gode and Sunder (1993) demonstrate that "zero intelligence traders" (who trade whenever they will not lose money) behave in a way that reasonably approximates the predictions of economic models in some experimental markets. Simple experimental markets are such strong environments that many different decision rules result in convergence to the equilibrium price.

Given such findings, support for an empirical prediction cannot be used to justify belief in the theory. While economically oriented scholars often assume that the rational explanation should be preferred when multiple theories make the same prediction (see Harwitz, 1998), any such preference is simply paradigmatic bias.

Prediction as the only test of a theory also deviates from our understanding of theories as explanations. The causal mechanisms figure centrally in what most of us think of as an explanation of behavior. While a given model might predict adequately, if we know the mechanisms are wrong, then the model is a poor explanation. For example, autoregressive models often predict well by simply curve-fitting the time series properties of data, but these do not explain the underlying phenomena nor do they offer sensible ways to influence the system. Few would see autoregression as a legitimate explanation for most phenomena.

Finally, if we wish to influence behavior (the third objective of strategic management research) the causal mechanisms that determine the outcomes matter. If we start with an incorrect causal mechanism, then our efforts to influence behavior will be misguided. For example, if we want to influence worker behavior, it may make a big difference whether subordinates follow the boss's instructions in response to incentives, norms, love, or fear.

The assumptions are close enough

Economists often respond to the behavioral critique by arguing that the assumptions are close enough that the logic holds. Lipsey and Lancaster (1956) discusses this in the context of social welfare economics – a branch of economics concerned with the welfare implications of various economic policies. Under the line of work known as the Theory of the Second Best, they demonstrate that, except under very stringent conditions, a logical argument has no bearing on any situation where any of its assumptions are false.

Specifically, if we know firms do not optimize, then we have no reason to believe a model based on optimizing has any relevance to how firms behave. Consider a physical analogy. Being on top of a mountain is analogous to making the optimum decision. Climbing a mountain is very different than being on top of one. If we assume we're right on top of the mountain (i.e., at the optimum), that is very different than what happens if we're a couple of feet off the ledge (just a few feet away). A small difference in assumptions can make a big difference in logical outcomes. Figure 3.1 presents one possible relation between an outcome and a choice variable. Picking the X that places the firm at the optimum differs radically from picking a slightly larger X.

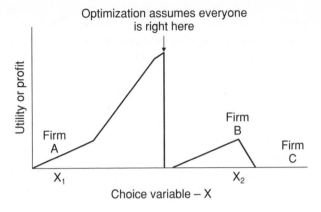

Figure 3.1 Optimization

However, even if we accept Friedman's argument for aggregate economic behavior, the problems strategic management researchers want to address (explaining firm behavior, explaining differences in firm performance, and suggesting ways to improve firm performance) involve firm or disaggregate behavior and outcomes.

If we assume strategic management research wants to explain differences in performance among players, and perhaps offer advice on how to win, then we must understand the internal mechanisms that generate the outcomes, not just predict outcomes. As Simon (1997b: 173) points out,

> the differential equations governing the bullet's flight are not supposed to represent the thought processes of a bullet, because a bullet does not have thought processes and its motion is not determined by thought processes. But the motions of human beings are determined by thought processes and we should not take much comfort or satisfaction from the billiard ball or bullet analogies or other analogies of that kind. If we want a theory explaining how people play billiards, we do not want a theory of perfect billiard balls; we want a theory of what heuristics a human billiard player uses in order to plan and make a (often not quite accurate) shot. These heuristics and actions do not involve solving the differential equations of the billiard board; they involve rules of thumb and it is these practice guides to action we are trying to discover in order to explain the behavior.

In the billiards example, *explaining outcomes by Newtonian mechanics points to the wrong thing*. It points to the direct movement of the ball, forgetting that the real problem, the difficult part of these games, is making the ball move the way you want it to move.

Likewise, the market reaction to a firm's products is only the way the ball rolls after it is hit. Firms and managers must choose the products to produce, design them, market them, produce them, etc. Each of these tasks involves uncertainty. Firm performance depends on an interaction of the outcomes on many task dimensions along with external market factors.

Given the same external conditions, actors will have different outcomes. Managers spend most of their time trying to improve results without changing external conditions – motivating, changing processes, etc. Much of learning pool involves getting the ball to go where you want it to go. Assuming optimal firm behavior or that pool players do not make mistakes (similar to assuming rationality) grossly handicaps our ability to understand competition or pool.

This comes back to a more general problem. If we are only concerned with aggregate behavior, it *may* be reasonable to use extremely poor assumptions or models of underlying micro-processes or behaviors.[12] However, if we want to understand the quality of a given performance, we need to understand the processes involved in that performance. Newtonian physics governs the good pool player and the bad pool player alike. Market forces influence the well and poorly managed firm alike.

Trying to explain outcomes or develop prescriptions from incorrect assumptions is like trying to do medicine with an incorrect understanding of anatomy and physiology. You may be able to predict some gross phenomena, but face severe handicaps in prescription or explanation at the individual level. Indeed, offering prescriptions based on mechanisms known to be incorrect verges on the irresponsible.

In strategic management, we want to explain who wins and perhaps suggest how they might improve. We certainly make similar claims when we teach classes in strategic management – implicitly (and sometimes explicitly) we claim that firms that follow the guidance of our texts and courses will generally perform better than firms that do not. Even if we allow Friedman's argument for its intended purpose, justification of the application of economics to aggregate behavior in economy, it does not provide an appropriate basis for understanding who wins in business competition nor for teaching how to win.

Very weak form rationality?

Faced with this kind of argument, one of my colleagues responded that rationality only requires sensible behavior *given the information people have deduced so far from the data.* Thus, he argued that finding a "day of the week" or "sunshine" effect in stock price data does not indicate non-rational behavior; it would only be non-rational if the phenomenon continued after the effect had been found.

This argument has three major problems: it contradicts normal economic usage, it eliminates much of conventional market theory, and it demands economics have a sophisticated theory of psychology. I will discuss this in terms of capital markets but the same logic applies to most efficient market analyses.

While one could use such a definition of rational, it conflicts with common usage in economics and finance. Conventional finance theory assumes rational decisions reflect all available data. The rational decision-maker must know all useful patterns in such data to optimally choose stocks. A standard test of efficiency or market rationality in finance is whether any patterns exist which would support strategies that could beat the market. The existence of such patterns is widely taken as demonstrating market inefficiency (Shleifer, 2000).

This new definition of rational is inconsistent with prior theorizing. Most capital market work assumes unbiased or rational expectations and optimal decision-making by investors. These result in a prediction that no investor will make abnormal returns based on publicly available data. These conditions are widely used to specify and identify capital market models.

Suppose there is an effect that has not been found, say abnormal positive returns occur on Monday. If investors do not know this, their estimates for Monday will be biased. If most investors have biased expectations, conditions exist where some investors could make abnormal returns (by appropriately timing the days).

Biased expectations and possibility of abnormal returns eliminate much of conventional capital market theory. Indeed, analyzing rational behavior requires strong assumptions about expectations – if expectations can have biases, then what rational behavior means becomes moot.

This "what they know" definition of rationality presents a third problem: accepting this definition of rational choice means economics needs a psychological theory of people's beliefs to make predictions based on rational choice. The advantage of rational choice assumptions is that they eliminate psychology and make choice a function of the facts of the environment. Making rationality contingent on "what people have deduced from the data" would force economists to have a theory of such deduction. Of course, economics has not been seriously concerned with such psychological issues.

Optimization is best!

Perhaps most annoying to a behaviorist, many economically oriented scholars assume an optimizing explanation is better than any other explanation unless you can clearly demonstrate that no optimizing model could possibly explain the phenomenon of interest.

As Kahneman (1994: 34) says:

> Thus a critic of the rationality assumption faced the following well-fortified position: (i) a definition of rationality which appears to be overly permissive in some important respects; (ii) a willingness of choice theorists to make the theory even more permissive, as needed to accommodate apparent violations of its requirements; (iii) a methodological position that treats rationality as a maintained hypothesis, making it very difficult to disprove; (iv) an apparent readiness to assume that behavior that has not been proved to be irrational is highly intelligent.

As one of my colleagues said, "given any behavior, I can think of a rational explanation."

Most rational explanations are simply goal-seeking explanations. Scholars advocating rational assumptions seldom if ever empirically demonstrate anything more than sensible reactions to the environment – they do not demonstrate rational (optimal) reactions. To find support for an optimizing position, we would need empirical tests that differentiate optimizing from other forms of goal-seeking behavior.

Alternative explanations should compete on an equal footing. To claim others must prove that rationality could not explain a set of data before entertaining another theory puts the onus on the wrong party. It arbitrarily makes rationality the null hypothesis to be accepted unless proven wrong, a disciplinary bias without logical justification.

Testing should not favor any particular theory. Explanations based on rationality, goal-seeking, routines, networks, or self-interest should all compete on an even footing. As Conlisk (1996: 686) notes, "evidence and plausibility should be the criteria, not prior bias toward optimizations."

Logical Problems of Rationality and Equilibrium

While rationality and equilibrium create general intellectual problems, they also create direct logical problems in strategy research. I have said little about equilibrium since more has been written about rationality as a basic assumption, but both are critical to many analyses.

If we assume agents or corporations always choose the best of all possible alternatives, then there is no need to study strategic management or have business schools. As Williamson (1985: 11) says, "[i]nteresting economic and organizational choices arise only in a limited (or bounded) rationality context." In a world where firms already make the right choice all the time, scholars cannot hope to add anything to practice. If firms were optimally run before business schools, then business schools have no real function.[13]

Assuming agents or corporations always choose the best of all possible alternatives also implies no progress has or can be made in management with the exception of progress due to new physical inventions. Rational firms must already act optimally. Thus, we must never observe an improvement in management practice from scholarly work in risk management, stock market investing, inventory management, operations research, production management, organizational behavior, etc.

Equilibrium offers equally desperate problems. A standard definition of equilibrium is that no individual actor can improve his or her situation by acting alone (Nash, 1950). Sargent (1993: 7) offers a similar definition that "[i]nsisting on the disappearance of all unexploited possibilities [for increasing utility or profits] is a feature of all definitions of equilibrium in economics." Asking how firms can improve if we start by assuming firms cannot improve (i.e., equilibrium) is absurd. That one might discover ways to improve management is inconsistent with the equilibrium assumption.

Both rationality and equilibrium are inconsistent with most of our research; we implicitly assume some firms make better decisions than others. If we really believed in rationality and equilibrium, then it is quite unclear what strategic management scholars should study (see below for Mosakowski's suggestions on this issue). Since all firms' choices are optimal responses to objective conditions, the choices seem of inherently little interest. By assuming rationality, industrial organization economics can ignore firm strategy and directly link market structure to performance. What would strategic management research mean under a theory that let us ignore firm strategies?

Faced with these problems, economically oriented scholars often try to casually lean on a behavioral perspective. Instead of assuming firms really are truly rational, they allow some noise. Instead of assuming markets are truly in equilibrium, they allow the possibility that firms might not be precisely in equilibrium. However, such modifications generally result in logical inconsistencies – a lack of rigor.

The optimization or equilibrium analysis assumes the firm is exactly at the optimum or equilibrium point. Consider the physical analogy of getting to the highest point of a mountain being analogous to reaching the optimum decision. A model that assumes we are sitting at the top of a mountain differs radically from a model of how to climb a mountain. Small deviations from the assumed situation (e.g., moving a few feet in either direction) can result in massive changes in outcome (see figure 3.1).

In trying to improve their organizations, managers may try to climb the mountain to the highest (most desirable) point. They do not know exactly where that point is, nor do they know the best route to that point. Any analysis that starts with the assumption that they have already reached that highest point (i.e., that they have optimized), will be totally misleading to their search.

The model of the highest point can also be misleading if the terrain is not simple. If one climbs a smooth, gentle mountain with only one peak (see position A in figure 3.1), strategies that say "go up" will eventually get you near the top (assuming you survive long enough and the environment stays stable). However, if the terrain is rough or contains multiple local peaks (local maxima), a hill-climbing process may never get to the highest peak because it finds a lower peak and does not see that there is anything better out there (see position B in figure 3.1). While this is a standard problem in optimizing functions using a computer, it has been applied to organizational adaptation as well (Levinthal, 1997). The local terrain might be flat, so small changes make little difference – this offers no reason to search further (see position C in figure 3.1). Even small complications in the model of learning (e.g., having two parties with biased expectations trying to find joint optima) can have devastating impacts on an organization's ability to learn in theory (Lounamaa and March, 1987) and experimental situations (Sterman, 1989).

In short, equilibrium and rationality assumptions offer substantial, fundamental problems to strategic management scholarship. In addition to the traditional critiques regarding theories with clearly incorrect assumptions, theories that assume optimality or equilibrium are inconsistent with trying to understand why some managerial decisions result in better or worse performance than others.

Before leaving this discussion of equilibrium and rationality, I should address one more canard – the claim by some that without equilibrium and rationality you cannot predict behavior. While I have seldom seen it written, I have heard it stated with conviction. Arrow (1986: S385–S387) also reports such a view:

> Let me dismiss a point of view that is perhaps not always articulated but seems implicit in many writings. It seems to be asserted that a theory of the economy must be based on rationality, as a matter of principle. Otherwise, there can be no theory . . . not only is it possible to devise complete models of the economy on hypotheses other than rationality, but in fact virtually every practical theory of macroeconomics is partly so based . . . the use of rationality in these arguments is ritualistic, not essential. . . .
>
> I believe that similar observations can be made about a great many areas of applied economics.

A variant on this argument says that, if we do not assume rationality, then we have irrationality and that cannot be predicted. As noted above, not optimizing does not mean "irrational" in the common usage; a mountain of papers use bounded rationality theories to predict (successfully) individual and corporate behavior. In some cases, rational models predict an inability to predict (e.g., in stock markets) while behavioral models make empirically correct predictions.

Some colleagues offer a similar argument about equilibrium: without equilibrium, we simply have noise. A weaker form of the argument says that without "equilibrating forces" the system will again be random. Just as some economists have trouble understanding an explanation of firm decisions without rationality, they also have trouble understanding an explanation of markets without equilibrium.

Economic models deal with equilibrium, not equilibrating forces. Arrow (1986) notes that, even with the assumptions for perfect competition, the theory of rational markets lacks a process for establishing the equilibrium. He argues that theorists who assume equilibrium have no theory to explain how rational actors should behave in a disequilibrium market. In other words, the "equilibrating forces" argument is ad hoc and not justified by the rational actor model.

Scholars talk about equilibrating forces instead of equilibrium to avoid claiming markets are in equilibrium. They want to retain the standard analyses from equilibrium assumptions without having to defend those assumptions. As discussed above, analysis assuming equilibrium has no meaning if we know the system is not in equilibrium.

Justifying an equilibrium analysis by the equilibrating forces argument is logically inconsistent. The assumption that markets are in equilibrium contradicts the assumption that forces push toward equilibrium but the market may not be in equilibrium.

If taken seriously, equilibrating forces implies a radically different kind of analysis than conventional economics – an analysis that takes such forces and adaptation seriously. A believer in rationality would need to explain why the market was not in equilibrium and to develop models of the process of moving to equilibrium. As Arrow notes, this largely has not been done and is technically extremely difficult in a rational framework.

Some implicitly assume that rejecting Nash equilibrium is to reject the influence of the environment on the firm. Nothing in bounded rationality models rejects firms searching for profits or environments influencing firms (and vice versa). Firms face complex environments that place a plethora of constraints on firm behavior. Indeed, the behavioral model of the firm recognizes more influences on the firm than the rational model – factors like norms, legitimacy, and conditioned ways of thinking along with conventional market issues. Firms interact in complex market systems. *This interaction strongly influences firm behavior, but does not have to lead to a Nash equilibrium.* Just as I can have incredibly stable behavior without rationality, I can have a wide variety of market behaviors without reaching a Nash equilibrium.

Social science is full of models that predict behavior but do not lead to Nash equilibria. Well-formed models can predict that things do not settle down to some stable value, instead continuing oscillation or random movement. Even if a model settles into a stable position, that does not guarantee the position is a Nash equilibrium – the stability could reflect people keeping the same behaviors as a result of rules, traditions, never having thought of the ways to improve their positions, or a misinformed belief they cannot improve their positions. Models of firms responding to market environments do not have to lead to a Nash equilibrium.

Behavioral models can deal with adaptation or equilibrating forces more easily than economic models, and indeed have. Let me offer one example.

Experimental economists often model and run experiments of simple markets where a set of sellers (with information on the prices at which they can obtain units of a good) and buyers (with information on what they will receive for the units) trade. The buyers and sellers transact in a simple market and, under many specifications, the market eventually stabilizes to the price predicted by economic theory. Equilibrium models only predict the final price and say nothing about the prices (and trades) before reaching the final price. While the trades before equilibrium are legitimate trades, economists generally ignore them since their theory says nothing about them.

Behavioral models can readily predict both a path to equilibrium, and the equilibrium. Gode and Sunder (1993) show that even "zero intelligence traders" will reach equilibrium, and their models predict the path to equilibrium. I once built an aspirations model where traders started with high aspirations (either a high or low aspired price depending on whether the actor trader was a seller or buyer) and then adjusted aspirations and offered prices until finding someone who would trade. This model converged to equilibrium and predicted the path to equilibrium. It actually converged somewhat more quickly than human traders. Behavioral models can predict the equilibrium or stable price and the path to that price. See Nelson and Winter (1982) for other examples.

To summarize, assuming rationality and equilibrium makes the entire endeavor of business scholarship and education questionable. Rejecting rationality in favor of other models of decision-making changes some predictions of behavior, but behavior remains predictable. Rejecting Nash equilibrium is not to reject the influence of the market, but rather to offer a different understanding of the market. The arguments of some economists imply that if someone rejects their model of the world (rationality and equilibrium), that individual accepts a model of total randomness. Firm and market behavior models do not need rationality or equilibrium to make sensible predictions.

Bounded Rationality in Economics

Following the critiques of Simon and others, substantial "bounded rationality" literatures have developed in economics, but these literatures define bounded rationality very differently than behaviorists. Two such applications that have influenced strategy research – agency theory and transactions costs economics – will be discussed later. Here, let me consider the issues more generally.

Bounded rationality models in economics usually model optimal decision-making subject to information constraints or costs. Instead of assuming the decision-maker knows everything and simply chooses, these models make the cost of finding information endogenous to the choice.[14]

Optimal decision-making subject to information costs differs radically from what Simon (1997a[1947]) defined as bounded rationality. Economic models of bounded rationality start with optimal decision-making and then introduce a small amount of either lack of knowledge (e.g., the principal in a principle-agent model doesn't know how hard the agent is trying) or information-processing costs. In contrast, behavioral models start with what people appear to know and work from there. An immense chasm lies between the two positions.

Consider a couple of examples from the economics literature. Carlton and Perloff's (1994: 557) industrial organization economics text says that "a sensible consumer processes information up to the point where the marginal benefit equals the marginal cost of processing more information (this behavior is called *bounded rationality*)." This is footnoted to citations to the work of Simon, Cyert and March, and Williamson.

Instead of a real bounded rationality model, this is an optimizing model incorporating some information-processing costs. As Arrow (1986) notes, such bounded rationality models attribute more computational power to agents than models that ignore information-processing costs. From a behavioral view, individuals cannot calculate the marginal benefit and the marginal cost of processing more information. A behavioral perspective recognizes that people do not know the expected benefits and expected costs of collecting additional information, nor do they do that kind of calculation. Instead, they rely largely on satisficing.

Sargent (1993) takes a strikingly similar position at the macroeconomic level. (Sargent, 1993: 21–2) begins by noting that the rational expectations paradigm

> imputes to the people inside the model much *more* knowledge about the system they are operating in than is available to the economist or econometrician who is using the model to understand their behavior. In particular, an econometrician faces the problem of *estimating* probability distributions and laws of motion that the agents are assumed to know. Further, the formal estimation and inference procedures of rational expectations econometrics assume the agents already know many of the objects that the econometrician is estimating . . .
>
> . . . We can interpret the idea of bounded rationality broadly as a research program to build models populated by agents who behave like working economists or econometricians . . . (italics in original)

Whereas rational expectations assumes all agents know the distributions of relevant variables, in Sargent's (1993) view of bounded rationality the agents must use the data to understand the world. Sargent assumes the agent has the same kind of knowledge and technical skills as the economist developing the model.

Oddly, Sargent ascribes this different conception of bounded rationality directly to Herbert Simon. As Sargent (1993: 22–3) says:

> Herbert Simon and other advocates of "bounded rationality" propose to create a theories [*sic*] with behavioral foundations by eliminating the

asymmetry that rational expectations builds in between the agents in the model and the econometrician who is estimating it. The idea of bounded rationality might be implemented by requiring that the agents in the model be more like the econometrician in one or more ways.

Instead of conceiving bounded rationality based on what real people know and can do with their information (as Simon clearly intended), Sargent assumes that all agents have the sophisticated understanding of economics and econometrics held by the most sophisticated economists and econometricians.

Part of the difference between economic and behavioral positions comes from an "anchoring and adjustment" process. Most economic models start with an extremely strong form of rationality. When scholars add bounded rationality to such models, they move a few steps from the traditional models. For example, the principal in agency theory knows everything except how hard the agent is working, and the agent knows everything (including the optimal strategy choices).

In contrast, a behaviorist starts with what appears to be the actual information-processing ability of the people of interest and adjusts to provide a manageable model. This implies simplifying our complex understanding to develop manageable models.

These radically different starting points result in economic and behavioral conceptions of bounded rationality differing radically.

Game Theory

While it has had only modest impact on the field of strategic management, in parts of economics, "strategy" largely means game theory. Indeed, Shapiro's (1989) paper titled "The Theory of Business Strategy" deals strictly with the application of game theory to industrial organization economics. Shapiro (1989: 125) claims that "game theory has emerged as the predominant methodology for analyzing business strategy." Despite its limited impact on strategic management, game theory's problems illustrate some important facets of the difficulties of importing economics into strategy.

Economically oriented scholars have debated the implications of game theory. Saloner (1991) argues game theory has little or nothing to say directly about strategy. He argues the problems managers face are too complex for the simple games that game theory has solved. Radner (1996: 1372) argues that "truly bounded rationality (uncertainty about the logical implications of what one knows), together with indeterminacy of equilibrium, make the current game-theoretic approach to the theory of the firm both implausible and inadequate." In contrast, Camerer (1991) argues that game theory should help strategic management research, and that many traditional criticisms of game theory are unfounded. In particular, he argues that many game theory solutions do not require substantial rationality and so should not be criticized for such.

This game perception of strategy raises a very critical difference between strategy and economic positions. Shapiro (1989) and others use the term business strategy to mean strategies to win within game theory. If a market does not present an interesting game-theoretical problem, then it has no strategic interest. Game theorists would immediately classify normal competitive markets as uninteresting since they do not present game theory problems.

From a behavioral standpoint, bounded rationality plays an immense role in making games worth playing. In economic game theory, chess is trivial: as it is a perfect-information, two-person, zero-sum game the players simply should write out all possible games (the extended form of the game) then choose the move that guarantees a win. The problem is that no one can enumerate all the possible games (estimates appear to suggest that there are approximately 10 to the 60th possible games, approximately the number of atoms in the universe). Chess is only interesting because we have bounded rationality.[15] Even when we use computers to play the game, we deal with limited computing machines. Von Neumann and Morgenstern's *Theory of Games and Economic Behavior* (1944) acknowledges this problem with game theory.

Consider an illustration from the game tic-tac-toe. With three-by-three cells, tic-tac-toe is a trivial game that few adults find interesting.[16] Once one sees the solution, one can guarantee a tie or, if one's opponent makes a mistake, a win. However, moving from three-by-three to five-by-five or ten-by-ten increases the complexity of the environment, and transforms a trivial child's game into a challenging intellectual activity. The size of the search space means we cannot solve the game as we have tic-tac-toe. Thus, we have sophisticated games such as Go, which essentially constitute tic-tac-toe with more cognitive challenge.

A game-theoretic analysis may be informative for games simple enough that individuals can manage the complexity. However, once the complexity increases beyond that which an individual can handle, the game-theoretic results become less useful. As a graduate student, one of my fellow doctoral students ran a political science experiment where individuals had sets of bills they wanted to pass, and they could logroll or bargain with other participants to get bills passed. Game theory predicted certain outcomes depending on the distribution of bills (interests) among the players and the rules for passage. The predictions worked well with small numbers of players and bills. However, a very sharp break point occurred where the number of players and bills exceeded the ability of the players to "act rationally"; after this point, the theory predicted poorly.

From a practical standpoint, the people who have actually learned how to program machines to play good chess come from cognitive psychology and closely related work in artificial intelligence, not game theory. This reflects that the important problem here comes from bounded rationality rather than the kind of problem game theory addresses. Economic game theorists can easily explain a general solution to the problem of chess, but that solution simply is computationally infeasible. Game theory without bounded rationality rules out the critical problem of how to work within computational constraints (bounded rationality).

Another part of my concern with game theory comes from a tendency of game theorists to make rather strong statements which may be correct within their terminology and framework, but which have uncomfortable implications outside those bounds. For example, based on a game-theory approach, Shapiro (1989: 127) asserts, "For investment to play a strategic role, it must be observable to rival firms. The investment also must not be recoverable. Costlessly reversible actions never constitute commitments and have no strategic role."

While this may be true in some models, it is not generally true. When a firm obtains an option on a new technology, this has strategic meaning even if the seller is willing to buy the option back at the purchase price. Competitors who know the firm bought the option will infer an interest in the technology. Furthermore, having that option changes the structure of any future interaction – competitors know the firm has access to that technology. Many activities that outsiders cannot observe have strong implications on strategic interaction in our terms. When it comes to playing out the game, these activities may not constitute a deterrent in game-theory terms, but they certainly can determine who wins.

Fisher (1989: 115) notes several problems with game theory applied to economics. First, some economists are happy to move from trivial games to policy advice:

> One, indeed, proposed to testify that in deciding whether to allow a merger in the petroleum industry, one should predict the effects on output and prices in terms of the change in the Cournot solution.

That, I think, is theory run riot. The petroleum industry does not consist of firms planning the one-time Cournot output-choosing game. Neither does any other real-life industry. That makes the one-shot game totally uninteresting.

He goes on to say that repeated games do little better. Citing the "so-called 'folk theorem'," Fisher (1989: 116) says:

Crudely put: anything that one might imagine as sensible can turn out to be the answer. While the folk theorem itself requires a number of assumptions, the existence of an embarrassingly large number of equilibria appears to be a fairly general phenomenon.

In addition to these general problems, game theory has two additional serious problems in strategic management:

1   Most problems we deal with involve excessively large search problems.
2   The winner is not solely determined by strategy, but rather by a combination of strategy, execution, and other skills. This includes the most popular games (football, basketball, hockey, etc.) as well as management. Totally ignoring skills and execution leads to a misleading view of the world.

Sen (1977) offers a very different critique of game theory, arguing that it assumes players are narrow-minded and unsophisticated. The rational actor in game theory acts solely in self-interest. Part of the reason for norms and morals is that rational self-interest may not be in the interest of the society. Addressing why people handle prisoner's dilemmas better than game theory predicts they will, Sen notes players may consider what type of preference they would like other players to have, and, following a Kantian analysis (see Bowie, 1999), see that the cooperative action has merit. Alternatively, individuals may act from what Sen terms commitment – actors sometimes do what they consider right even if it is not in their self-interest.

Game theory offers a misleading perspective on strategy. It defines strategy to be problems solvable by game theory rather than problems of corporate direction. It ignores many if not most of the important issues. While simple game theory models may offer insights, they cannot form the basis of strategic management. Generalizing from game theory to strategic management may be misleading.

A Lack of Rigor

Economically oriented scholars sometimes claim economic modeling provides rigor and that this is a substantial advantage over other work in the behavioral sciences. I would argue that economic work in strategy is often less rigorous than behavioral work.

A rigorous piece of work should be clear about its assumptions and maintain coherent and logical connections between the assumptions and all the subsequent analysis, including the data analysis and prescription if one engages in such activities.

Strategic management work that assumes rationality and equilibrium tends to lack rigor. Assuming firms act rationally as conventionally defined implies there should be no systematic procedures that give competitive advantage – "no rules for riches" (Barney, 2001; Mosakowski, 1998). Obviously, we cannot systematically look for rules that explain differences in firm performance within a theory that says such rules cannot exist.

On a similar note, economic work often describes the conditions of some hypothetical optimum and then casually assumes that somehow those conditions are relevant to firms and competition away from that equilibrium or optimum. Climbing mountains is different than sitting on top of mountains.

Finally, as argued above, any logical argument clearly implies its assumptions. Most economic analyses avoid testing or even recognizing their assumptions could be tested. Thus, they ignore the inconvenient predictions of their analyses.

Economic work often is rigorous in some of its activities but at the expense of lacking rigor in other areas. Just as experiments have high levels of internal rigor, but become questionable when the results are applied in the field, optimization or equilibrium models can have complete internal rigor, but their application to substantive problems in the field may lack rigor.

Uses of Formal Models

While some uses of economic theory come from careful application of economic models, many more come from casual use of what scholars perceive to be general conclusions of economics. For example, Mosakowski (1998), Barney (2001), and Rumelt, Schendel, and Teece (1991) present the "no rules for riches" conclusion as a general truth. Let us consider some issues regarding the formal versus informal use of theory.

Formal rational firm theory can be used in different ways:

(a) As a formal model – working through the mathematics of the models in the context of interest. This use provides the most power and is the most consistent with formal modeling logic. If one's assumptions are correct, it is least likely to give erroneous implications.
(b) As a general guide. Here we take the general implications of a set of models and use them as guides.
(c) As a metaphor that helps illuminate a problem by showing its similarity to other things.

These issues arise in both normative and positive theorizing. Normative work attempts to derive prescriptions while positive work attempts to explain behavior.

I will use the application of options theory to strategic management as an example. In options, one makes an initial investment to buy the right or possibility of making a decision later. For example, when someone buys a call option on a stock, the holder receives the right to buy that stock at a specified price up until the date the option expires. The value of an option goes up with the price variability of the underlying stock because that variability positively influences the likelihood that the stock will exceed the specified price (and therefore make the option valuable).

Normative and positive applications of rationality contrast oddly. In a positive application, the user assumes the firm acts rationally and uses this assumption to predict behavior.[17] For example, assuming the firm makes decisions according to options theory predicts some firm behaviors. In a normative application, the user assumes the firm will be better off if it makes its decision following a rule derived from rational analysis. For example, it assumes that using an options formula will improve a firm's capital allocation. The normative application assumes, contrary to the positive application, that the firm was not acting optimally before.

For either application of a formal model to a real situation, the user must verify that the environment fits the assumptions of the model. For example, to use options pricing models in strategic applications, the assumptions made in deriving the mathematical models should be true of the strategic context.[18] The legitimacy of the models rests on these assumptions.

Lest the reader think this is an odd behaviorist requirement, note that options advocates justify options models over net present value (NPV) models precisely because the assumptions of the options models fit the reality better than the assumptions of the NPV models. They argue that conventional NPV analysis assumes only one decision made early in the process and so gives misleading results in problems where managers gain information over time and get to make additional decisions.

In strategy, we see many applications of the (b) or (c) sorts. Instead of presenting a specific mathematical model, scholars take the general implications of a theory and apply them without carefully working out the mathematics in a given situation, or use the models as metaphors. These applications run the very real risk that the assumptions of the model are not checked for their fit with the real world.

Let me deal with (c), metaphorical use, first since it is simplest. People may use models as guides suggesting things to examine or ways to frame a problem. Using models as metaphors provides value by offering different ways of thinking about a problem, not by providing a "correct" tool. For example, options thinking tells the manager that current decisions create the potential for later decisions and that at the later time only the positive courses need be taken. Particularly to managers who have been forced to analyze R&D investments from an NPV perspective, this reframing can be incredibly useful. In this case, whether the model has been carefully elaborated in a given context is irrelevant to the value generated, although the general structure of the problem must match the theory.

Strategy scholars often do analyses of type (b) – taking results from a model and using them directly. Both prescriptively and descriptively, this creates difficulties.

Prescriptively, such application raises questions. Since the application does not carefully match the assumptions of the theory to the situation, the model may or may not give a good answer. For example, we do not know if options pricing models generally give better answers to real problems than normal human judgment. We have some cases where models greatly improve on human decision-making (e.g., in scheduling tasks), and others where humans dominate models (e.g., in repeated prisoner's dilemmas). I suggest that those who advocate a tool should demonstrate the effectiveness of the tool as directly as possible, rather than rely on faith based on the tool's theoretical background.

We have similar problems in positive applications. The major danger here comes from repeating conclusions from theoretical models as fact without questioning whether the models really fit the context. Taking such conclusions as facts can mislead subsequent theorizing and our interpretation of empirical results. This usage is particularly dangerous when the conclusions are almost unconsciously accepted. For example, an analysis might take the theoretical argument that competitive markets imply zero rents as fact without checking whether the markets of interest meet the extremely stringent conditions by which the theory defined a competitive market (and checking whether firms do make rents).

When pushed about the realism of their assumptions, economically oriented scholars often fall back to something similar to item (b) – a general provision of insights. As one of my friends said, "We were told [in an economics doctoral program] that the important thing is not the models per se but the insights that they give you that is important." This would be fine if the insights were in fact used for casual discussion. Scientific debate demands a higher standard. That is, this argument justifies a model the author acknowledges is mis-specified because it leads to insights about an external situation. But, to rigorously assess whether the model's insights apply to the situation, we must assess whether the assumptions of the model fit the situation.

Perhaps I over-interpret "insights" – if insights only means jogging the memory or offering ways to see things (the metaphorical application of type (c)) then the rigorous assessment is irrelevant. However, if this is all one wants, then there is no reason to favor formal models over brainstorming or synectics or any of a hundred methods offering new ways to see things. Those who rely on formal models present them as more than creativity aids.

This use (b) of general rules from models is problematic. Economically oriented scholars sometimes offer things as true based on theory rather than empirical evidence. Let me offer some examples:

1   Several scholars in strategy have published the "no rules for riches" statement.
2   Our friends in finance teach that stock price equals the net present value of future earnings or dividends and their models often assume this is true. Easton's (1985) empirical findings indicate this is wrong – stock price systematically and substantially deviates from the net present value of dividends and earnings.
3   Others advocate economic value added (EVA) to measure performance because it resembles theories of capital market valuation, but the empirical evidence shows traditional measures explain stock returns better than EVA (Biddle, Bowen, and Wallace, 1997).
4   Finance scholars teach net present value is the right way to evaluate capital investments. We have no research showing firms that use this technique do better than other firms. Indeed, such research would not interest top finance journals. They believe their theory so much that they do not need to test it.[19]

Some economists assume that showing a theory is inconsistent with global rationality is equivalent to showing the theory is incorrect. As Simon (1997b: 22) says:

An interesting sequence recurs frequently in the literature on unemployment. Shortly after any new theory is published on this topic, another article appears showing that the unemployment predicted by the new theory only arises because one of the economic actors is behaving with less than global rationality (recall Keynes' emphasis on the money illusion of workers, or Lucas's on the money illusion of businessmen in explaining the under-employment of resources). This observation that the theory incorporates bounded rationality is regarded as refuting the theory. Of course, it does not refute it. What it does is simply raise the empirical question of whether the limit of rationality postulated by the theory is present in the real world. This is a question to be decided by evidence, not by applying the assumption of global utility maximization.

This logic appears in the finance literature where models that create the possibility of arbitrage have been rejected on a theoretical basis without bothering with the empirical facts. Or, as Shiller (1986: S502) says, "[t]hose who bring up such a possibility [of fads in capital markets] are viewed as if they were bringing up astrology or extrasensory perception."

In practice, scholarly work in economic models offers an excessive appearance of generality. Papers present the development of a model as a natural, logical progression from a set of supposedly reasonable assumptions to a set of conclusions. However, the actual process of model-building does not resemble the final output.

When scholars build quantitative models, they often try various assumptions to find ones that lead to interpretable, tractable, and sensible outcomes. However, when they present the results, they do not present them as "a set of assumptions exist in which this is true" but rather they state their results as if their assumptions were the only reasonable ones (see the Viale (1997) quote above). Furthermore, they often state the results as facts, not as hypotheses to be tested.

For example, Shleifer (2000: 27) describes a model that "describes the interaction of noise traders and arbitrageurs and shows that in cases where arbitrageurs trade in anticipation of noise trader demand they move prices away from rather than toward fundamental values." That one can build a model with this outcome is important and interesting. However, rather than showing what it claims to show (an empirical assertion), it really shows that one can build models where this is true. The economics literature is full of equivalent statements where building a model where X is true is described as "X is true."

From a strategic management standpoint, I agree with Saloner (1991) that formal modeling provides stories or guides rather than proofs. In many cases, the importance of the model is that it provides a logical reason for a given empirical observation. However, this has two serious drawbacks. First, many scholars think that demonstrating such a logical path mathematically is better than showing it verbally. This simply reflects a disciplinary bias toward mathematical models, often with relatively obvious conclusions. Second, some scholars treat such a mathematical proof as an *empirical* proof when it is really only a proof of the possibility. As one example among many, Amihud and Lev's (1981) influential empirical paper on risk reduction as a motivation for corporate mergers rejects the possibility that an owner whose entire wealth is invested in a single firm might want to diversify the firm's holdings. Their rejection comes from a utility maximization model, not from empirical findings about owner behavior.

In short, we must not casually accept findings or proofs constructed within a given theoretical framework or apply them until we validate that the framework fits the empirical world.

Summary

This chapter criticizes assumptions of equilibrium and rationality in strategic management. These assumptions contradict the possibility of achieving the goals of strategic management research as identified in chapter 1 – explain firm behavior, explain differences in firm behavior and performance, and offer suggestions for improving firm performance. They also have little or no empirical support. Indeed, where empirical evidence does exist, it demonstrates that these assumptions are incorrect.

While one might reject my arguments as the ranting of a behaviorist, please note that many of the primary points echo statements of outstanding economists – Arrow, Baumol, Simon, etc. As Douglass North (2001) says:

> The rationality assumption just conceals all the interesting questions that we have got to try to understand if we are going to do better at understanding the way in which economies, policies, and society evolve through time. If we want to ask where institutions come from, how they evolve the way they do, we have to ask ourselves another set of questions. We have to move to cognitive science. We have to ask ourselves questions that relate to the problems of how do people make choices in the face of uncertainty. If we do not ask that question, then we are not going to get any further than simply assuming away almost all of the interesting problems we have to be concerned with. In particular, when we ask ourselves how the process of change in society works, we are not going to get anywhere because the process of change begins with the way in which, in human

beings' minds, they construct and understand an explanation of the world around them.

Having discussed the problems with equilibrium and rationality assumptions, I now turn to a behaviorist evaluation of current work in strategic management.

Notes

1   This chapter draws heavily on Bromiley and Papenhausen (2003).
2   For a very different critique, see Hirsch, Friedman, and Koza (1990).
3   Those interested in this debate might examine Sen (1970, 1977), Kornai (1971), and Hollis and Neil (1975). In the management literature, a recent contribution is Zey (1998).
4   Too many papers reject expected utility to survey here. Let me mention one odd example. Utility theory assumes somewhat stable utility functions. Wilson and Daly (forthcoming) find that showing young males pictures of "hot" women changed the males' discount rates (a form of utility for future rewards) for unrelated financial transactions. The data suggest a similar effect for women and "hot" cars.
5   For example, prior to choosing which Ph.D. program to apply to, few if any budding scholars collect detailed information on all Ph.D. programs. Furthermore, none predicts the content and probabilities of all the possible future career, intellectual, and social outcomes contingent on their selection of a program.
6   Knight (1954: 10), who is famous for his contributions to understanding uncertainty in economics, says: "one fact about man is that he is a romantic and opinionated animal rather than inclined to truth-seeking or fact facing. A rational being – indeed! He says so himself as a compliment, hardly meant as truth. People will have answers, even to questions that make no sense; and they will 'do something' – will 'monkey' where they do not understand. They demand absolutes, and there is none – truth no exception. . . . Typical of man is one extreme or the other – to be marvelously intelligent or amazingly stupid – and well satisfied with himself in either role . . . P. T. Barnum made fame and fortune on the maxim that the public loves to be swindled . . . Voltaire said his clearest idea of infinity came from observing the credulity and gullibility of the human race."
7   Even the Catholic Church only claims the Pope is infallible on matters of doctrine.
8   Rational models can justify non-optimal behavior by firms. For example, an agency theory analysis with misaligned CEO incentives predicts CEOs operate in sub-optimal ways from the owner or corporate perspective (Jensen and Murphy, 1990). This will be discussed in the section on agency theory.

9   As Robert Marris (1997: 138) says, "we are a particularly bad example of the possibility of theories persisting which certainly do not fit the facts very well. More and more evidence comes that the theory is not a very good theory and yet the theory persists because of ideological or other intellectual properties that it may have . . . in the last twenty years, it [economics] had actually moved away from being scientific, it had become more theoretical, more sophistic-ated econometrics had become better and better, and yet I believe economics as such has become, in a deeper sense, less scientific."

10   An important distinction between behavioral and economic approaches comes in the treatment of assumptions. While economic work often rejects the idea of empirically testing assumptions, behavioral work assumes that assump-tions should be factually correct and subject to testing.

11   Sen (1970) notes that rationality predicts few should vote if they do not derive direct pleasure from the act of voting. Assume, as public choice economists assume, that voters vote to increase their expected returns, which depend on which party is elected (i.e., they vote in their self-interest). The probability of a given voter's vote determining the election is extremely small. Thus, unless the electoral outcome would immensely change the voter's personal situation, the expected utility of voting will be less than the utility the voter can obtain by using the time elsewhere, so few will vote.

12   I do not believe this, but it is not germane to the issue in strategic management.

13   The discussion below concerning the "no rules for riches" statement expands on this point.

14   Agency models handle bounded rationality differently. They assume the principal does not know a specific thing (how hard the agent is working) and then solve for optimal actions contingent on that ignorance.

15   Some believers in optimization have argued that situations where individuals clearly try to come in first have some implications for whether people optimize. In chess, people clearly try to win, but clearly cannot optimize. Just because I want to win does not change the fundamental constraints of my intellectual apparatus – I am still boundedly rational at best and play chess ineptly.

16   Except of course those in academic administration. A word to the wise: a nice inlaid tic-tac-toe board is always a tasteful gift for a Dean or Associate Dean.

17   See Miller and Shapira (2003) for experimental evidence that even individuals trained in options models do not follow the models' prescriptions.

18   Fisher Black, who generated the most common model for evaluating options, told a colleague of mine that he thought that applying his model to real op-tions was misguided since real options did not meet the necessary conditions.

19   I do not know how good these tools are. I do believe that when someone says, "Use this hammer, it is the best hammer," the consumer can legitimately ask for empirical evidence that it drives nails better than other hammers. Shouldn't it worry you when they have no evidence?

4 | A Behaviorist's Perspective on Current Strategy Approaches

This chapter deals with two issues. First, it briefly reviews strategy research streams that explicitly or implicitly take a behavioral view – population ecology, cognitive processing, top management teams, decision-making, and traditional content research. This section reminds the reader of the substantial behavioral literature in strategy. Second, it considers several areas of strategy research that take either partially or fully rational approaches – rules for riches, the resource-based view, transaction costs, and agency theory. This section discusses the problems rationality and equilibrium assumptions create for these theories.

Behavioral Traditions in Strategy

Research in strategic management has profitably drawn on a number of different perspectives. This chapter demonstrates that several of these perspectives share common behavioral foundations.

A given theory can generate multiple models by changing parameters or ancillary assumptions. The behavioral view fits naturally into several main areas of strategic management research: population ecology, top management teams, managerial cognition, networks, and much of strategy content work.

This section points out how many strategy studies share fundamental behavioral assumptions. I have chosen not to review these areas in depth – given my opinion that the majority of strategic management research has relied on behavioral assumptions, such a review would require reviewing almost the entire field. Instead, I suggest the reader simply look carefully at strategy research published in the top journals.

Population ecology   explains the structure of a population of firms by focusing on firm births and deaths. Hannan and Freeman (1977, 1984) argue that selection environments favor firms with high structural inertia, which equates to having stable routines. Hannan and Freeman (1984) say that firms must have reliability and accountability. Actors in and outside the organization demand dependable and predictable behavior from the organization. Workers want to know jobs will be there. Lenders want to know they will be repaid. Customers want to know the firm will be around to service what it sold. Investors want their investments used the way they thought they would be used. Suppliers favor dependable customers. Reliability is rewarded and reliability equates to stable routines.

Indeed, Hannan and Freeman (1984) are quite consistent with the behavioral theory of the firm and emphasize the roles of organizational routines in their arguments. As Amburgey, Kelly, and Barnett (1993) say, "following Hannan and Freeman (1984), we define organizations as structured systems of routines embedded in a network of interactions with the external environment." Amburgey and Miner (1992: 335) start with, "For nearly 30 years observers have argued that inertia pervades organizational life (Cyert and March, 1963)."

By including the "network of interactions with the external environment" Hannan and Freeman (1977, 1984) extend the behavioral theory of the firm to include a number of more recent organizational theories. They note that firms need legitimacy – appropriate publics must see the organization as legitimate or they will not support it. Furthermore, firms are embedded in networks of relations. Overall, Hannan and Freeman's view of the organization resembles Cyert and March's behavioral theory with no adaptation of routines.

Later work has begun to examine change with an emphasis on the costs and difficulties of change (see e.g., Amburgey, Kelly, and Barnett, 1993; Amburgey and Miner, 1992). The behavior of a population of firms changes both by existing firms changing and by the founding and death of firms – learning and selection. The underlying model of the firm in these studies again strongly resembles the behavioral theory of the firm.

Industrial organization economics work and the population ecology approach share one important similarity – they both look to the environment and number of competitors as the primary factors in determining outcomes. However, they take conflicting positions on critical factors. Within industrial organization economics, the environment and number of competitors determine outcomes because firms adapt optimally to their environments.

In population ecology, the environment and number of competitors determine outcomes because firms cannot change.[1]

Industry organization economics and population ecology also differ in their understandings of time. Assuming market equilibrium in the economic approach implies firms and populations change quickly. In contrast, population ecology's emphasis on birth and death focuses heavily on disequilibrium or unstable periods. Carroll and Harrison (1993, 1994) used parameters from population ecology studies of newspapers to predict that such unstable periods can last hundreds of years.

Population ecology takes a behavioral approach to the organization and competition. While optimizing models can justify some inertia based on investments in current activities, when those activities become unprofitable the investments should be treated as sunk costs. Optimizing firms adapt to their environments, whereas the population ecologist's firm adapts very slowly if at all due to substantial structural inertia. Population ecology offers an extensive set of studies demonstrating how behavioral assumptions can apply to competition.

Managerial cognition falls naturally with the behavioral approach. Indeed cognition and bounded rationality fit together completely. From the earliest work (e.g., March and Simon, 1958), bounded rationality scholars have emphasized the importance of beliefs and perceptions.

Work on managerial cognition takes several forms. Some scholars study ways to improve managerial decision processes by directing conflict (e.g., Schweiger, Sandberg, and Rechner, 1989). Some studies demonstrate and explain how managerial perceptions differ from objective evaluations of the situation (Meindl, Stubbart, and Porac, 1996; Sutcliffe and Huber, 1998). Others examine specific psychological patterns such as self-serving attributions (attributing good outcomes to one's efforts and bad outcomes to exogenous forces) and their influences on firm performance (e.g., Clapham and Schwenk, 1991). Others examine how changes in managerial interpretation influence strategic behavior (Barr, 1998; Barr, Stimpert, and Huff, 1992).

The cognitive perspective's application to cognitive groups merits comment. The strategic groups literature had been strongly criticized because traditional methods of identifying groups relied on archival accounting data and then attempted to explain other archival accounting data. By having managers identify close competitors, scholars can identify strategic groups using data that are completely separate from accounting data (McNamara, Luce, and Tompson, 2002; Reger and Huff, 1993). This lets them study how perceptions of strategic groups influence strategic behavior and performance.

Top management teams.   The substantial literature on the constitution and process of top management teams (TMTs) rests on a behavioral foundation. This literature argues that the TMT plays a pivotal role in directing the corporation. Thus, the quality of the TMT's decisions should substantially influence the performance of the corporation. This requires a behavioral perspective – TMTs must differ in the quality of their decisions for TMTs to be interesting.

Because data on top manager functional backgrounds, sex, age, education, and years with the corporation were readily available, early research emphasized such demographic variables in explaining performance. However, the theorizing employed information-processing or group process mechanisms. For example, researchers argued that cognitive diversity increases the ability of the team to understand and adapt to changing environments. They then used demographic diversity as a proxy for such cognitive diversity.

Recent studies deal more directly with the underlying constructs regarding TMT processing. For example, Simons, Pelled, and Smith (1999) examine how trust within the TMT influences the relations between conflict and performance. Rau (2001) examines the impact of TMT's knowledge distribution and knowledge sharing on bank performance.

The TMT literature inherently requires a behavioral perspective. While agency theory has been applied to top managers in corporations, it does not explain demographic or process variables influencing behavior. The rationality assumptions of most agency arguments rule out the possibility that individuals differ in expertise since the rational decision-maker always chooses the optimal choice. TMT composition and process only matter if some TMTs make better decisions than others, implying non-optimal decisions.

In short, the TMT literature parallels the cognitive literature in directly examining information-processing in strategic management. Both literatures treat TMTs and firms as information-processing entities. They draw directly on cognitive and organizational behavior research.

Organizational decision-making   includes a variety of different research streams, all of which take an essentially behavioral approach.

One stream, exemplified by Fredrickson's work on strategic decision processes (Fredrickson, 1984; Fredrickson and Iaquinto, 1989) and Eisenhardt and Bourgeois's work in high-velocity environments (Bourgeois and

Eisenhardt, 1988; Eisenhardt, 1989) examines how general characteristics of firm decision processes influence firm decision quality and performance. These studies clearly demonstrate that strategic decision processes influence firm performance, and the appropriate decision process depends on the firm's industry.

Another stream examines firm risk-taking based on theories of behavioral decision theory and organizational decision-making. Work here includes Fiegenbaum and Thomas's (1986, 1988) work on risk-return associations, March and Shapira (1987), and a variety of studies my students and I have done. Some have extended these firm-level studies to examine specific risky decisions (McNamara and Bromiley, 1997). See Bromiley, Miller, and Rau (2001) for a review.

A third stream uses theories of organizational decision-making to explain corporate decisions such as radio station format changes (Greve, 1998) and R&D activities (Fleming and Bromiley, 2002). See Greve (2003) for a review of this literature.

All the decision-making work shares a behavioral foundation.

Social networks research looks at information and other flows based on who deals with whom. Recent work has begun to differentiate carefully among kinds of networks and what transmits over a network (e.g., friendship versus business information) (Bell, 1999; Bell and Zaheer, 2001).

Social networks fit largely within a bounded rationality model of behavior. Information, rather than transferring rapidly as in most rational actor models, transfers through networks. Decisions depend not just on self-interest, but also on the entire realm of social interactions defined by networks.

In addition to these specific areas, behavioral concepts have been widely applied in the literature. For example, trust has taken an important place in understanding numerous organizational and inter-organizational phenomena (Bromiley and Cummings, 1995; Zaheer, McEvily, and Perrone, 1998; Zaheer and Venkatraman, 1995).

Traditional content research. Finally, a large body of strategy content research implicitly takes a behavioral approach. This work makes sense from a behavioral standpoint, but is grossly flawed if one assumes rationality.

Take the classic strategy question of diversification. Assume for the moment there are no lags or adjustment costs (this simplifies the discussion but does not change the structural issues). The immense majority of this literature examines associations between diversification and firm performance. It assumes diversification influences performance.

This makes sense if firms choose diversification patterns and some firms choose better than others. If scholars do not know the best diversification pattern for a given firm, we can hardly expect that all managers will pick the best pattern given their firms' conditions. Managers in firms often disagree strongly over diversification moves, implying the correct move is not obvious. Furthermore, no plausible mechanism exists by which managers would learn the optimal diversification pattern for their firms – conditions change too quickly, the patterns are too complex, and the relations depend on too many variables.

Assuming firms make optimal choices transforms the diversification issue. If firms have chosen the optimal diversification given their situations, diversification then is a mediating variable between the true factors (the firm's situation) and performance. Any relation between diversification and performance must first be attributed to prior, perhaps unobservable, differences that influenced the diversification choice.[2]

Assuming firms make optimal choices makes it difficult to interpret a statistical association between diversification and performance – since the optimal diversification has been chosen, the theory implies that any change (whether positive or negative) from the observed level of diversification for a given firm must lower performance. An analysis across firms of the relations between some independent variables and diversification could characterize optimal diversification (under the rather strong maintained assumption that all firms have optimal diversification). Data on firm performance does not tell us much. While normally we would use it to estimate what would happen to a firm's performance if its diversification changed, under optimal diversification assumptions both increases and decreases in the independent variables must negatively influence performance.

Assuming firms optimize shareholder returns implies that changes in diversification should have ex ante positive expected value. Many changes in diversification involve mergers. The literature indicates that on average acquiring firms lower their shareholder value by acquisition. This implies that firms make acquisitions that have negative expected values.

Some have tried to explain this in a rational model by arguing top managers have incorrect incentives. If this were true and this powerful (i.e., that large numbers of firms take on large numbers of acquisitions with negative expected value), then we should discard the model of the firm as maximizing shareholder value. Instead of a model of firms maximizing shareholder value, we would need a model of firms slowly destroying shareholder value by actions with negative expected returns. After all, if the incentives are so bad they cause acquisitions that on average have slightly negative value, why should they be better for any other corporate action? Indeed, acquisitions should be better controlled than most corporate activities – boards of directors must directly approve most acquisitions.

Roll (1986) blames managerial hubris. He argues that managers systematically overestimate their abilities and so make ill-advised acquisitions. Almost all the optimizing literature assumes reasonably accurate expectations (usually unbiased); it is hard to explain why a rational decision-maker would have biased expectations. Furthermore, without a theory to predict the biases in expectations, allowing biased expectations means a rational model can predict almost anything. See Hayward and Hambrick (1997) for a behavioral study on managerial hubris.

In contrast, a behavioral view offers models that predict biases in managerial expectations. The behavioral decision theory literature strongly supports the view that individuals have great difficulty generating statistically valid analyses. Managerial forecasts demonstrate strong and consistent biases (Bromiley, 1987). Indeed, in many management systems, everyone assumes everyone biases their forecasts. Not only are biases in managerial expectation a reasonable part of a larger behavioral research tradition, behaviorists also have the tools and willingness to directly examine the problem. For example, one could ask whether firms that make better acquisitions really have more accurate forecasts than those that do not.

Most diversification research in strategic management implicitly takes a bounded rationality view. Consistent with bounded rationality, it finds some firms make better diversification decisions than others, and that diversification influences performance.

While I have talked at length about diversification and acquisitions, the same kind of issues occur for other areas of content research. For the most part, strategy content scholars have taken an implicitly behavioral approach. I recommend they explicitly recognize it.

Summary of behavioral streams. The majority of research in strategic management implicitly or explicitly makes behavioral assumptions. While in economics and finance economists can legitimately ask what non-optimizing research would look like, strategic management's behavioral research tradition dates from its earliest years and provides the majority of the findings in the field.

Having briefly noted research streams that rely on behavioral assumptions, I now turn to several issues and theories that have taken at least partially rational actor approaches to strategy.

No Rules for Riches?

Let me begin discussing the implications of economic logics for strategy with a minor, but important, conclusion strategy scholars have taken from economic analysis: the "no rules for riches" statement.

Rumelt, Schendel, and Teece (1991), Mosakowski (1998), and Barney (2001) all say you cannot have rules for riches – there can be no rules that generally will assist individuals or corporations to increase their financial returns. Barney (2001: 50) says, "If the application of a theory to a firm without any special resources can be used to create strategic advantages for that firm, then it could be used to create strategic advantages for any firm and the actions undertaken by any one of these firms would not be a source of sustained competitive advantage."

If there really are no rules for riches, strategic management scholars are in trouble. Empirically, we should never find systematic patterns associated with better or worse decisions. Furthermore, there should be no possibility of prescriptive results since prescriptions are rules for riches. Note that we have a very strong statement made by five outstanding scholars regarding no rules for riches.

I understand "no rules for riches" as implying that no rules exist which will improve the performance of any identifiable group of firms (unless those firms have special resources).

"No rules for riches" comes directly from assumptions of rationality and equilibrium. If firms make optimal decisions, then there can be no better decisions, which implies there can be no rules that yield better decisions. Likewise, if markets are in equilibrium, firms cannot make themselves better off. This directly implies there can be no rules that would make firms better off. It also implies that no such rules can be invented – otherwise the firms were not making optimal choices.

While the simplest justifications of "no rules for riches" come directly from definitions of rationality and equilibrium, some justifications argue that if someone finds a rule, then others will copy it, and once enough firms copy it the rule will provide no benefits. This justification is somewhat convoluted and requires numerous assumptions regarding how others learn and adopt the rules. In practice, performance-enhancing rules often take long periods to be adopted. Many firms still could benefit from basic operations research applications to scheduling, inventory management, etc. TQM and Taguchi techniques were documented in English but American managers ignored them for decades. The empirical evidence clearly rejects a general assumption that productive rules transfer quickly.

"No rules for riches" directly parallels finance theory logic. Conventional financial analyses (assuming rational investors and market equilibrium) predict no rules for riches. A standard test for market efficiency in finance is whether any rules exist which can beat the market, i.e., produce abnormal returns. In weak form efficiency, it means no rule can beat the market using publicly available data. This includes both known and unknown rules. Many of the studies searching for rules that can beat the market have found them (see Shefrin, 2000; A. Shiller, 2000; Shleifer, 2000; Thaler, 1993). Even in capital markets, many rules have been found to beat the market.

"No rules for riches" is problematic for strategy scholars since we hope to understand why some firms perform better than others. If we found a pattern of behavior that leads to high performance and other firms could profitably adopt this pattern, we would have a rule for riches. Assuming no rules for riches rules out the possibility of explaining differences in firm performance by systematic patterns associated with better and worse choices.[3]

Mosakowski (1998) offers a very rigorous and innovative attempt to address this problem. Much of her paper challenges the proposition that goal-setting increases expected returns for firms. She does this because the existence of any practice that generally improves performance for firms would empirically refute the "no rules for riches" claim. She tries to demonstrate that the current goal-setting literature does not provide indisputable evidence of positive returns from goal-setting. She clearly recognizes that the entire "no rules for riches" story would be refuted by empirical evidence of rules that increase firm performance.

Of more theoretical interest, she develops a justification for managerial decisions in an environment where there are "no rules for riches." She assumes that managerial choices all have identical expected values. If potential choices vary in expected value, then rules that identify high expected value options could offer positive returns. Mosakowski argues that much of the RBV prescriptive literature is not helpful to managers. She notes that telling managers to find important resources but ones they cannot understand is somewhat confusing guidance.

Similar to Lippman and Rumelt (1982), she assumes the outcomes from decisions have some stochastic component. A given decision may have a probability of high returns (riches) even though the expected return is 0. Lippman and Rumelt modeled this possibility of riches as a draw on a distribution where higher values give positive returns.

Since, by assumption, managers cannot find choices with high ex ante expected values, she recommends that they look at the distributions of returns rather than the expected value. She says, "[t]o understand the impact of managerial prescriptions, we must know the shapes the distributions associated with alternative managerial choices" (Mosakowski, 1998: 1179). She assumes that, although managers cannot change their average returns, they can change the distributions.

This radically transforms the objective of the corporation. Normally, we assume firms try to increase accounting performance or returns to stockholders. This means firms can influence the expected value of performance. Assuming all investments have equivalent expected values implies that managers can only influence the distribution of potential outcomes, not the expected value.

Instead of attempting to increase expected performance, her firm maximizes "the cumulative probability associated with earning any positive rent level" (Mosakowski, 1998: 1170–1). If managerial choices cannot influence expected performance then managerial choices should never explain average performance. Risk becomes the only interesting issue in the field.

The fallacy in the "no rules for riches" story is the assumption that everybody learns everything. Consider any skilled activity, for example playing bridge or chess. Many books offer guidance on improving performance in such activities. The books offer the novice player clear rules, which definitely can help performance. Perhaps the very best competitors know the existing rules and are sufficiently skilled that no new, simple rules exist to help them. However, rules exist that can help the immense majority of players. If rules can help players in the simple world of chess or bridge, we should assume rules may help in the far more complicated management world.

In other words, the "no rules for riches" story falls down because it assumes economic rationality where firms rapidly and optimally learn all available rules. In contrast, most studies of organizational learning find surprising difficulties are encountered in even simple things like transferring technologies within a given firm. Knott (2001) finds firms rapidly quit using valuable rules (practices that positively influence performance) when they leave a franchise system, despite already having implemented the rules. Likewise, studies of factory productivity find substantial and durable differences in productivity across the factories in a given industry. McKinsey (1993) often finds over 50 percent productivity differences between most and least efficient producers in several industries. Several literatures demonstrate that firms are slow to adopt desirable innovations. After all, *half the firms in any industry would be better off being average.*

Empirically, numerous scholars have found rules for riches. The quality movement appears to have positively influenced performance for its early adopters. Scholars have attributed the performance of many Japanese companies to their management techniques, techniques that were publicly documented. Various operations research and process management techniques have clearly improved performance – many firms can still benefit from operations research analyses of inventory, production, or distribution systems. Firms that organize appropriately as defined by transaction cost theory appear to perform better than those that do not (Armour and Teece, 1978). Agency scholars and others who study incentives claim that proper incentives improve performance (and that many firms do not have proper incentives). In addition, an immense collection of strategic management scholarship suggests various ways in which firms could improve their performance. From both a theoretical and an empirical standpoint, the evidence is overwhelming that techniques exist that could improve the performance of many firms.

A believer in "no rules for riches" might answer this criticism by saying that these examples only come from industries that are not in equilibrium. This is true by definition – if unused rules existed that could improve performance then the industry cannot be in equilibrium. This defense runs into two problems. First, the scholars who say "no rules for riches" often omit the caveat "in a world that is in equilibrium." They offer the statement as a general truism. Second, if we add the equilibrium caveat, then we need evidence an industry is in equilibrium before we apply "no rules for riches." However, we lack evidence that any industry is in equilibrium. Thus, the statement describes a hypothetical situation, which may never exist in real life, but has been offered as if it described all industries everywhere.

The "no rules for riches" argument exemplifies the way assumptions of rationality and equilibrium can cause problems for strategic management scholarship. While Mosakowski (1998) does an outstanding job trying to deal with the problem, in a rationality and equilibrium world no satisfactory solution exists. However, this did not stop several outstanding strategic management scholars from reiterating this shibboleth as truth. Simply taking such conclusions from other disciplines can lead strategic management astray.

The Resource-Based View

Individuals entering strategy who wanted to maintain a largely economic perspective faced some unpleasant facts. While the industrial organization economics tradition had some explanatory power, it said little about performance differences within industries (or industry groups). The data strongly demonstrated that firms in similar businesses differed significantly in performance, and such performance differences often continued for many years (Mueller, 1977). The challenge was to explain durable performance differences without giving up much of the micro-economic framework.

The maintenance of an economic flavor was critical to this problem. Strategic management had a long history of considering inter-firm differences. Indeed, the classic statement of the Harvard strategy view, Andrews's (1971) *The Concept of Corporate Strategy*, mainly discussed factors that differentiated firms. However, the traditional Harvard view suffered from two major problems. First, it seemed correct but did not lend itself to scientific testing (a problem that some claim the RBV shares, see Priem and Butler, 2001a, 2001b). Second, it did not phrase the problem in economists' terms. However, the RBV has a very close resemblance to Andrews's theory; asked at an Academy of Management session how the RBV advanced on Andrews's arguments, Jay Barney described the RBV as "old wine in new bottles."[4]

To highlight the change in their thinking, some scholars have claimed that most strategic management work in the 1980s focused on industry-level analyses and that the RBV restarted the field doing firm-level studies. For example, Barney (2001: 54) says, "I also believe the 1991 article was helpful in reintroducing firm attributes into strategic management research after a period in which work focused almost exclusively on industry determinants of firm performance." Levinthal (1995: 20) says, "In early work, the focus was on distinctive competencies among firms . . . the primary interest became diversity across industries . . . the field is now in the process of re-adjusting its focus to firm-level differences under the rubric of the resource view of the firm." Other scholars made similar statements (cf. Dierickx and Cool, 1989; Priem and Butler, 2001a).

As Bromiley and Fleming (2002) demonstrate, this is incorrect. Even a casual perusal of the tables of contents of *Strategic Management Journal* demonstrates that industry-level analysis never formed more than a small fraction of strategic management scholarship. Table 4.1 presents the titles of the articles from the first issues of *SMJ* in 1983, 1984, 1985, and 1986. I chose the first issue each year simply to keep the number of papers reasonable. Given Porter's book appeared in 1980 and Wernerfelt's original resource-based view paper appeared in 1984, I would have thought these were the top years for industry analysis.

From the titles, we see that only one (number 15, "An Application of Clustering for Strategic Group Analysis") of the 21 papers is a study of

Table 4.1 Article titles from *Strategic Management Journal*, 1983–1986

Volume 4, number 1 (1983)

1. Effectiveness in Marketing Planning
2. A Diagnostic Framework for Planning
3. The Visible and the Invisible Hand: Resource Allocation in the Industrial Sector
4. The Trade-off between Production and Transportation Costs in Determining Optimal Plant Size
5. Technological Evolution and Competitive Response
6. Business and National Priorities for Industrial Development: Intersectoral Consensus in Israel

Volume 5, number 1 (1984)

7. A Concept of Entrepreneurial Strategy
8. Influence of Public Affairs Offices on Corporate Planning and of Corporations on Government Policy
9. Neurotic Style and Organizational Pathology
10. A Strategic Planning Network for Nonprofit Organizations
11. Manufacturing Strategy: Defining the Missing Link

Volume 6, number 1 (1985)

12. Redirecting Research in Business Policy and Strategy
13. Managers' Conservatism and Corporate Performance
14. Managing the New Venture Division: Research Findings and Implications for Strategic Management
15. An Application of Clustering for Strategic Group Analysis
16. Competitors' Responses to Easily Imitated New Products – Exploring Commercial Banking Product Introductions

Volume 7, number 1 (1986)

17. Towards a Contingency Theory of Corporate Planning: Findings in 48 U.K. Companies
18. Diversification: The Growing Confusion
19. Networks: Between Markets and Hierarchies
20. Entrepreneurship and Paths to Business Ownership
21. Environmental Analysis Units and Strategic Decision-Making: A Field Study of Selected 'Leading-Edge' Corporations

industry determinants of firm performance. Only two others could possibly be concerned with industry analysis – number 6 ("Business and National Priorities for Industrial Development: Intersectoral Consensus in Israel") and number 12 ("Redirecting Research in Business Policy and Strategy"). Number 6 is actually "a survey of experts chosen from Industry, Labour, and Government in Israel, who ranked and scored three business and four national goals in the context of industrial development." Number 12 argues that "[d]eductive theorizing, with more attention to a game-theoretic definition of equilibrium and to recent ideas from economics, should be one new direction for policy research." In short, only one of the 21 articles addresses industry determinants of firm performance.

I do not know how one could describe one out of 21 articles as the "primary" or "almost exclusive" focus. Wondering if my sample period was too early, I examined the first issues of *SMJ* for 1987 to 1992 and found at most five of 40 papers dealing with industry analysis. Whether one in 20 or five in 40, industry analysis papers clearly did not constitute an "almost exclusive" focus! Perhaps economically oriented scholars only read the industry analysis papers, but *these papers were never more than a small fraction of the published research.* Historically, most strategic management scholars have focused on inter-firm differences in behavior and performance that were not associated with an industry emphasis. I leave a full explanation for this substantial misrepresentation of scholarly history to the reader.

Returning to the substantive issues, Lippman and Rumelt (1982) attempted to explain why firm profits could vary in equilibrium by developing a model where firms drew production functions from a random distribution. The firms that drew the best functions had durable positive returns.

Barney (1986, 1991) addresses the problem posed by Lippman and Rumelt: how can firms have differing performance levels in equilibrium?[5] He generally assumes firms optimize. He provides an outstanding attempt to generate a model that assumes firms act optimally but have performance differences in equilibrium. (See Bromiley and Fleming (2002) and Priem and Butler (2001a, 2001b) for more detailed critiques.)

In the following discussion, I will refer to the RBV as laid out in Barney (1986, 1991). I use these articles because they offer some of the clearest and most rigorous developments of the RBV. These are solid articles – I disagree with their assumptions and objectives, but they offer fine analyses.

The RBV assumes some firms have scarce resources that other firms do not. These resources are not just traditional capital and labor, but rather include a variety of skills and intangible abilities. The firm is defined as a bundle of such resources. For such resources to have value in equilibrium, competitors must be unable to imitate the resources (called uncertain imitability). Furthermore, since firms could hire away a profitable firm's managers, the firm's managers cannot understand their resources.[6] With these assumptions, and assuming firms act optimally, the RBV offers a very clean tie between "resources" and "performance":

$$\text{Resource} \Rightarrow \text{Performance}$$

To directly tie resources to performance requires assuming that firms make optimal decisions – they use their resources to optimize returns. Without this assumption, we would need to understand how firms decide to use their resources and to recognize the actual returns from a resource could fall below those potentially available in other applications.

Note the inconsistency in use of rationality assumptions. To justify intangible resources remaining with a firm, firms must have bounded rationality in that they do not understand their resources. However, to justify an equilibrium assumption, firms must use their resources optimally, i.e., rationally. Thus, firms must optimally exploit something they do not fully understand – a very curious idea. This is consistent with Heiner (1983) and others, who note that the empirical regularities being explained by optimization models often would not exist if firms acted rationally. The assumption about not understanding resources follows exactly the tradition discussed previously of making arbitrary assumptions to facilitate rational theorizing.

RBV work developed two very different intellectual streams. What Levinthal (1995) called the "high church" approach followed Barney in taking equilibrium and rationality assumptions seriously. Another stream takes a more behavioral standpoint – what Levinthal called "low church."

Some RBV scholars assume rationality and equilibrium while others do not. This creates massive difficulties for building a coherent theoretical structure. While theoretical work may progress with different scholars making different ancillary assumptions, that scholars differ in basic assumptions invites confusion. RBV scholars do not agree on basic issues like the definition of resources – *the* central concept of the theory.

I will present a behavioral approach that offers an alternative intellectual foundation for predictions of the RBV sort.

A behaviorist might parse the problem as follows. A firm is a complex system that includes physical assets, routines, intellectual and financial assets, knowledge and skills of management and employees, etc. The firm's outputs can be described along numerous dimensions (cost, quality, etc.)

and these can be compared across firms. A given firm may do some things better and others worse than competing firms. "Better" means in ways that increase profitability, normally through increasing the customer's likelihood of purchase and the price the product can command, or reducing costs. A given organizational routine could have some outputs that help performance in a given market and others that hurt performance there.

In contrast, RBV scholars describe the firm as a bundle of resources. This is a very misleading image. Complex organizations are complex systems, not bundles.

The distinction between describing a firm as a system or a bundle of resources is substantial. A system can have complex interrelations. A system can have multiple inputs and outputs. Individuals in a system can evidence loyalty, apathy, and a host of other behaviors. Describing firms as systems connects our work to organizations' scholarly community. Describing firms as bundles of resources contradicts what organization theory has learned about organizations. The bundle image suggests you can choose whatever things you want from the bundle. Often this is incorrect – you have a set of processes and the processes can be described in various ways. Most firms have some features management finds useful and some that management would love to eliminate. The "bundles of resources" description also appears to exclude all the features of the firm that do not have specific impacts on performance. If resources are rare, then the "bundles of resources" definition excludes most of all firms, and perhaps all of some firms.

A behavioral perspective complicates the tie from resources to performance. By assuming all firms use their resources optimally, the RBV eliminates the importance of strategic choice. It also largely ignores the influence of product markets (since everyone picks the best possible market).

Instead, a behavioral analysis would assume that the mix of things the firm can do and the markets in which it chooses to compete influence firm performance. Furthermore, firm returns depend on all the behaviors of the firm in the markets in which it competes, not on one single "resource" such as customer service or innovation.

Graphically, the behavioral view might look like the diagram in figure 4.1. The firm is a system and its outputs have characteristics. Management makes choices that influence the system and influence how and where to compete. Performance then depends not just on the positive characteristics of the firm's system (what some call resources) but also on the negative ones, the choice of market, competitors' actions in that market, and customers' actions. This opens up a number of realistic possibilities. For example, a firm can be great at something, but compete in a market where

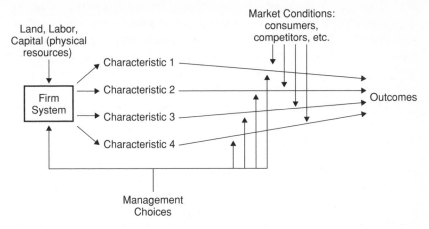

Figure 4.1 Characteristics, choices, and competition: a static view

that capability is not valued. This diagram and our discussion to this point are largely static. At any given time this may be true – in the short run, a firm is stuck with its processes and its management choices.

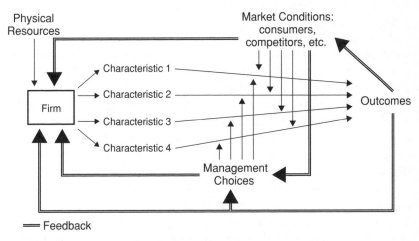

Figure 4.2 Characteristics, choices, and competition: a dynamic view
Source: Bromiley and Papenhausen 2003: 426.

Unlike the resource-based view, the behavioral approach easily addresses adaptation and change as well as static relations (see figure 4.2). As Nelson and Winter (1982) note, optimizing perspectives have inherent problems in explaining and dealing with change. The behavioral theory of the firm addresses in depth how feedback influences managerial choices and organizational change. Feedback should change managerial choices and the behaviors of the organization. Furthermore, firm behaviors influence customer demand and other market characteristics so the market and competition change over time as well.

To explain performance differences in equilibrium, the RBV requires that even firms that have resources do not understand them so that other firms cannot steal these resources by hiring managers away from the focal firm.

Rather than this strange assumption (that firms optimally use something they do not understand), let us assume that if a firm does something particularly well, other firms may try to copy it. Learning is by no means as easy as the RBV suggests. Assume some firm behaviors positively influence a firm's performance. Before competitors can mimic these behaviors, the competitors must recognize that the behaviors have value. Some firm characteristics that increase performance may not be copied simply because the competition does not see the value of those particular characteristics. Given heterogeneous customers, dozens of characteristics that may influence customer choice, thousands of activities that add up to the cost structure, the likelihood that these factors interact, and limited variance in many factors, understanding how firm behaviors influence firm performance is not trivial.[7]

Once competing firms understand the value of a behavior, they must replicate it. An odd contrast exists between the technology transfer and RBV literatures. The RBV assumes anything not nailed down transfers. This is why the RBV argues that managers must not understand the source of their resources.[8] In contrast, scholars who study technology transfer emphasize the difficulty of transferring skills. The literature contains many cases where firms have difficulty transferring skills within their own organization, let alone copying those skills from an uncooperative competitor (Szulanski, 2000).

The technology transfer literature helps us with this problem. Retaining valuable skills is the inverse of ease of technology transfer about which we know a great deal. Codification aids transfer. Ability to observe the behaviors aids transfer. Framing the retention of profitable skills as a problem in avoiding technology transfer lets us take advantage of the technology transfer literature. This gives us an empirically justified foundation for understanding transfer instead of ad hoc assumptions. It also frames the question as transfer rates rather than the RBV's extreme assumption of zero transfer.

If the RBV is flawed, then why is it empirically supported? Simply, much of the research that references the RBV does not test it.

Many empirical studies ostensibly in the RBV literature mention the RBV to justify looking at differences across firms but use a different theory to derive their hypotheses. For example, Zaheer and Zaheer's (1997) outstanding study of competition in global currency trading refers to RBV, but uses network theory to justify its hypotheses. Priem and Butler (2001b) cite numerous papers where researchers paraphrase or cite Barney's work but do not define their terms in the original RBV terms. Barney (2001: 46) admits that many of the empirical papers that cite his RBV papers do not test the theory, but rather the RBV is "used primarily to help establish the context of some empirical research, for example, that the focus is on the performance implications of some internal attribute of a firm."

When scholars do try to directly test the RBV, they face two very different concepts of performance: sustainable competitive advantage and abnormal returns in equilibrium (see Foss, 1997). Lippman and Rumelt (1982) and Barney (1986, 1991) deal with returns in equilibrium, but this is a difficult concept empirically. Returns in equilibrium would require demonstrating a market is in equilibrium and then measuring returns. Despite its central place in economic logic, we have no empirical standards to determine whether an industry is in equilibrium. Instead, RBV scholars talk about sustainable competitive advantage.

Profits in equilibrium and sustainable competitive advantage have no necessary relation. I could have a sustainable advantage in a market with long-lived disequilibrium. For example, industry structures adapt slowly, making it quite possible for an industry to have a disequilibrium structure. Alternatively, I could have profits in a short-lived equilibrium. Finance theorists assume stock prices are in equilibrium, but those prices (and equilibria) change almost continuously. Profits in equilibrium and sustainable competitive advantage are quite different.

Furthermore, it is hard to measure sustainable competitive advantage. Measuring competitive position in a way that differentiates it from profits is difficult,[9] but assume we can use financial performance as a proxy for competitive position. To measure sustained competitive advantage, we would need a measure that identified *firms with sustained above-average performance*. That is the construct. We would want to explain the differences between these firms and all others, and (perhaps) explain differences within the group with sustained above-average performance.

Conventional performance measures (return on assets, return on equity, stock returns), whether annual or averaged over years, do not measure sustained above-average performance. Clearly, you cannot use data on firms with below-average performance as if they were on a continuum of sustained above-average performance.[10] While half the firms in a sample have above-average performance, most of them have above- and below-average performance years that average out above average. Such firms do not meet the sustained criterion. The observations for firms with sustained competitive advantage will be quite limited – only a small fraction of firms has sustained high performance (see Wiggins and Ruefli, 2002).

Why should we be interested primarily in sustained competitive advantage? After all, *half the firms in the industry would be better off being average.* The other half may be more interested in increasing average performance than reducing variance (i.e., in high average performance rather than sustainability). Our theories of appropriate firm financial objectives emphasize the expected value of income flows, not their lack of variation. Conventional financial economics assumes firms should maximize the expected value of net cash flows and not care about the unsystematic variation. Understanding those few who sustain high returns is certainly interesting, but it cannot stand as the general objective of strategic management research.

I suspect scholars who emphasize sustained competitive advantage and profits in equilibrium implicitly assume an equilibrium world where everyone earns normal returns except those with resources. The traditional efficient market model has everyone earning normal returns and then the RBV gives those with resources higher returns. In such a world, it makes sense to differentiate between normal firms and those with resources. However, the empirical distribution of firm returns does not match this description. Firm return distributions vary widely by industry and seldom evidence a "normal return" cluster.

Finally, it is not clear that the RBV makes interesting predictions (Bromiley and Fleming, 2002; Priem and Butler, 2001a). The RBV suggests that firm performance should differ and be correlated over time, but any sensible model makes these predictions.

Supporters of the RBV claim that it predicts something about market imperfections and performance. For example, some RBV analyses attempt to test the RBV by seeing if firms that purchase in imperfect factor markets can differentially perform (e.g., Poppo and Weigelt, 2000). One might assume that purchasing in imperfect factor markets should let some firms have abnormal high performance. This is not implied by conventional economic theory. According to economic theory, if we buy in a perfect market, we will pay the equilibrium price. When firms buy in an imperfect market, economic theory implies *the possibility exists for the buyer or the seller to make abnormal profits, and for the other to have abnormal losses!* We cannot predict whether the seller or buyer will gain the advantage without additional assumptions concerning the details of a particular imperfect market. We could also have an imperfect market where neither could obtain advantage. Without specifying the imperfection, that a market is imperfect leads to no predictions about the returns to a given participant in that market.

In recent years, some scholars have started to emphasize dynamic capabilities or dynamic RBV (Helfat, 2003). Without delving deeply into this literature, let me note that, as Nelson and Winter (1982) argue, rationality and equilibrium assumptions make sensible dynamic analyses difficult. Furthermore, when including bounded rationality, scholars who emphasize economics often make inconsistent or arbitrary assumptions. For example, Foss (2003) argues that this work ignores how individuals' bounded rationality influences firm routines. A fully behavioral approach would offer greater consistency than an ad hoc mix of behavioral and rational analyses.

To summarize, the RBV attempts to solve a very difficult but incorrectly formulated problem – developing a model that gives profits in equilibrium with rational firms. Followers of the RBV often implicitly vary from the rationality and equilibrium assumptions, leading to a jumble of inconsistent arguments. The behaviorist view offers several advantages over the RBV.

First, the behaviorist view recognizes that the things a firm does often come from complex processes – 3M's positive resource of innovation comes at the cost of a negative resource of high overhead costs. Thus we replace this curious abstract image of the firm as a bundle of resources with a much more realistic picture of the firm as a complex organization where we may describe its outputs on various dimensions.

Second, the behaviorist view recognizes that many things a firm does lack intrinsic value but rather interact with other organizational activities to contribute to the value the firm creates by competing in a given market. By calling the characteristics resources, the RBV associates them with our normal usage of resources (labour, money, etc.). However, the RBV resources differ from normal resources because markets exist for most resources but not for most RBV resources. Thus, we can meaningfully discuss the value of a restaurant or a factory, but we cannot do this with the RBV's uncopyable, not understandable, intangible resources. Equating the two kinds of resources makes the RBV's ephemeral resources appear concrete.

Third, firms don't always pick the optimum market and market strategy to use a given ability: bounded rationality implies people seldom if ever do anything optimally. Furthermore, to compete in a given market often requires multiple capabilities. For any given firm and market, the firm may have some capabilities that fit the market well and others that the market does not value.

Finally, a behavioral view places transfer of information and learning back into a sophisticated theory. Whereas RBV analyses assume that everyone learns everything if anyone understands it, transferring skills and capabilities can be difficult. The degree of difficulty and such problems have been extensively studied in a variety of literatures.

Some of the things one would get from this behavioral view of competition resemble work that some have labeled as RBV-based, but which avoids the problems of the RBV.

The RBV versus Porter's industry analysis

The two main approaches to strategic management research coming out of economic foundations, the RBV and industry analysis, offer interesting contrasts in their use of economics.

Traditional industrial organization economics assumes firms make optimal decisions given the structure of their environments. Thus, structure drives conduct which drives performance. However, assuming optimal conduct given structure lets scholars in this tradition move directly from structure to performance.

Porter's book on five forces analysis handles the problem of economic assumptions very nicely by largely ignoring them. Rather than attempting to draw clear scholarly lines between industrial organization economics and strategic management, Porter takes a far more metaphorical and empirical approach. Whereas the theory assumes that environments fully determine firm behavior, Porter simply looks at the characteristics of the environment that lead to performance and asks how firms can obtain environments with those characteristics. He thus translates the empirical findings (which do not depend on optimizing or efficient market assumptions) into strategy without importing the other assumptions.

Contrast Porter's exercise with the RBV, which tries to more carefully tie itself to neoclassical economics. By drawing such ties, the RBV creates logical and empirical problems (see the section above) that cast substantial doubt on the RBV approach.

Porter's approach offers a model for understanding how strategy scholars can use economic findings. The empirical findings of economists often stand independent of the theoretical assumptions. For example, an empirical finding that the number of competitors in a market negatively influences performance would not require the specific assumptions about market efficiency – this is an empirical finding.

However, the Porter approach leaves us without a solid theoretical foundation. Many of his recommendations (even that he offers recommendations) imply that firms did not make optimal choices. I consider a behavior approach to competition in the final chapter of this book.

Transaction Cost Economics

Transaction cost economics (TCE) offers an interesting blend of behavioral and economic assumptions. It generally assumes bounded rationality – individuals cannot forecast the future well, and cannot write perfect contracts. On the other hand, it assumes that firms adopt optimal organizational structures.

TCE rests on three assumptions: bounded rationality, opportunism, and asset specificity (Williamson, 1975, 1985). Bounded rationality implies firms cannot forecast perfectly, nor can they write complete contracts. Opportunism means firms will lie to advance themselves, termed "self-interest seeking with guile." Asset specificity means that investments can create positive returns within a given transaction but have little value outside that transaction. The basic problem is that efficient operation may require investments that have little value outside that operation, but the parties cannot trust one another, nor can they write a perfect contract. Thus, for transactions with high asset specificity, bringing both parties to the transaction into the same company (internalization) may be more efficient than doing the transaction in a market.

The opportunism assumption merits some criticism. Rather than seeing honesty as a variable, TCE takes the conventional economic position that people will be dishonest whenever it is in their interest to do so (Bromiley and Cummings, 1995). Williamson's position justifying the no-trust assumption can be summed up as, if you cannot tell who is trustworthy and who is not, you must treat all as untrustworthy.

Systems to control opportunism have costs so the appropriate expenditure on controlling opportunism depends on the costs of control compared to the potential outcomes without those controls. With partially trustworthy agents, then, the appropriate level of control will generally be less than the level if we assume complete opportunism.

For example, suppose we want to design a control system. If we are managing a population of nuns, most of us would design a less sophisticated control system than if we are managing a population of hard-core criminals. Stores and gas stations certainly design more or less trusting systems depending on their location and clientele. In many areas, you can pump gas and then go into the store to pay. In others, you must pay before you pump. Most liquor stores are self-service, but in particularly dangerous areas the liquor and employees are behind protective glass. The sensible control system depends on the expected losses from not having the system compared to the cost of the system and expected losses from having the system. These vary across populations. While situations may exist where we cannot assess how trustworthy others are whatsoever, most business situations allow some assessment.

Bromiley and Cummings (1995) offer hypotheses based on TCE logic but assuming that trust varies. For example, trust should mitigate the impact of asset specificity in vertically related production systems, reducing the need for vertical integration. Within organizations, trust should increase the creation of inter-divisional joint projects.

The second problem with TCE comes from inconsistency in its bounded rationality assumptions. Williamson assumes bounded rationality when it comes to writing contracts but assumes global rationality when it comes to selecting governance arrangements. He says, "[a]ll complex contracts are unavoidably incomplete by reason of bounded rationality," but "transaction cost economics ascribes foresight rather than myopia to human actors" (Williamson, 1999: 1089). Assuming that all firms adopt optimal governance arrangements largely eliminates the choice of governance arrangements as an explanation for performance differences (see Mosakowski, 1991). It also is inconsistent with bounded rationality. To assume managers who never learned TCE knew how to structure governance according to TCE principles *even before Williamson discovered those principles* conflicts with a bounded rationality assumption.

While we might expect that, on average, over time, selection and adaptation favor organizational structures well suited for a given kind of transaction, this differs radically from assuming all managers know the right structure.

Indeed, Armour and Teece (1978) find exactly the kind of adaptation a behaviorist would expect. Early adopters profited from moving to the M-form while late adopters did not. Assuming that firms optimally choose organizational form creates problems here. If the innovation had value at the beginning of the analysis, why did it not have value earlier? Why did the late adopters not adopt earlier? While the obvious explanation is that the companies had not thought of it, this is inconsistent with assuming that firms make optimal structure choices.

Overall, TCE follows a largely behavioral approach with the major exception of assuming that firms know the right structure. Being openly behavioral about the discovery and transmission of good governance arrangements would strengthen TCE. Instead of assuming that firms know all possible arrangements, a behavioral position would say they have to learn about arrangements. Desirable physically possible arrangements are not used because managers have not thought of them. After invention, desirable organizational forms may diffuse through the economy. Organizational technology diffuses in organizational populations just as mechanical and electrical technologies do.

Before leaving the TCE discussion, an exchange between Simon (1991) and Williamson (1999) merits comment. Simon (1991: 27) claims TCE has not been properly tested, with the result that "the new institutional economics and related approaches are acts of faith or perhaps of piety." Williamson (1999: 1091) strongly rejects Simon's conclusion, noting the "number of published studies exceeds 400 and involves scientists in Europe, Japan, India, Mexico, South America, New Zealand, and the list goes on . . . the theory and evidence display a remarkable congruity."

This exchange reflects differences between Williamson and Simon on appropriate theorizing and testing. Before the "acts of faith and piety" passage Simon says that both agency theory and TCE take an essentially optimizing model of the firm and individual (with ad hoc bounded rationality assumptions), and add many additional assumptions to it. As Simon (1991: 26–7) says,

A fundamental feature of the new institutional economics is that it retains the centrality of markets and exchanges. All phenomena are to be explained by translating them into (or deriving them from) market transactions based on negotiated contracts, for example, in which employers become "principals" and employees become "agents". Although the new institution economics is wholly compatible with and conservative of neoclassical theory, it does greatly multiply the number of auxiliary exogenous assumptions that are needed for the theory to work. For example, to explain the presence or absence of certain kinds of insurance contracts, moral risk is involved; the incompleteness of contracts is assumed to derive from the fact that information is incomplete or distributed asymmetrically between the parties to the contract. Since such constructs are typically introduced in the analysis in a casual way, with no empirical support except an appeal to introspection and common sense, mechanisms of these sorts have proliferated in the literature, giving it a very *ad hoc* flavor.

In general, the new institutional economics has not drawn heavily from the empirical work in organizations and decision-making for its auxiliary assumptions . . .

Here lies the difference in concepts of empirical support. When Williamson talks about empirical support, he means that the general predictions are roughly correct. For example, asset specificity and uncertainty correlate with moving transactions into firms rather than markets. When Simon talks about empirical support, he means that the internal mechanisms and assumptions of the theory need empirical support, either from prior empirical results or by direct testing within the context of the theory.

Simon's (1991) concern also comes from having an alternative theory to explain the aggregate results. Agency theory and TCE assume self-interested and amoral individuals. Simon (1997b), Sen (1970, 1977), and others argue that organizations of strictly self-interested individuals would not function. Instead, they offer other explanations for organizational cohesion and cooperation, including identification and pride in work (see also Tyler, 1999).

If employees are completely self-interested and get no pleasure from their jobs, control mechanisms will elicit insufficient cooperation from individuals for organizational functioning. Academics offer a good example. If all faculty members simply did what directly and tangibly paid off for them personally, we would find no mentoring, no service, and little collegiality. Where teaching (measured by student satisfaction surveys) figured into pay and promotion, instructors would tailor courses strictly to student satisfaction. Where it did not, courses would be designed to minimize instructor effort. Everyone would use multiple choice exams rather than essays or short-answer exams. For senior faculty over whom the school has almost no leverage, we should see terrible teaching and no service whatsoever. After all, senior faculty are seldom dismissed for lack of service (just doing service duties badly is enough to get out of them), or for bad teaching, and at the end of a career the pay incentives available to most faculty are trivial.

The problem is not just academics; formal incentives only deal with part of any job (see Simon, 1991). If employees really just do the minimum required by the rules (a work to rule – an effective labor tactic that stops production in many systems), or only what is rewarded, most organizations cannot function. If employees were fully self-interested and amoral, managers could do little – even firing would not help since the new employees would be just as self-interested and amoral as the old.

Coming back to testing TCE, we have two very different explanations why internalization helps in certain circumstances. Williamson argues that organizations provide more effective controls than markets for exchanges where contracts are hard to write and enforce. Simon (1991, 1997b) argues that the benefits largely come from employees identifying with the organization, not just from controls (see Kogut and Zander (1996) for a similar argument).

Most tests of TCE do not differentiate between these explanations – *they do not test the causal mechanism*. Instead, they relate the difficulty of the contracting problem (asset specificity, uncertainty) to organizational arrangements. Few studies test why the organizational arrangement works.

Both from scholarly and practical perspectives, it makes a big difference whether internalization works because it provides good control over self-interested, amoral employees, or because it provides employees with a sense of identity with the organization. While I suspect both operate, I know of little or no evidence on the point. Good empirical work tests the mechanisms of the theory. Here it would explore how these two very different explanations operate.

Agency Theory

To run an organization *entirely* on incentives to personal gain is pretty much a hopeless task.

The *purely* economic man is indeed close to being a social moron. Economic theory has been much preoccupied with this rational fool decked in the glory of his *one* all-purpose preference ordering. (Sen, 1977: 336, italics in original)

Individual motivation plays a central role in many theories. In economic work, it has its foremost development in agency theory. In organizational behavior, it has been studied for decades under the label motivation. Everyone agrees that motivation and incentives influence behavior.

Agency theory addresses the problem of getting a subordinate to act in the principal's interest, i.e., to act as a good agent for the principal. Most agency work assumes a risk-neutral principal who cannot tell whether the agent is acting in the principal's interest. It assumes a risk-averse agent who knows the right things to do, but acts strictly in the agent's self-interest. It assumes that agents will lie but principals do not. It assumes that performance depends on both agent behavior and random factors.

These assumptions lead to a focus on incentive and control systems that align the subordinate's interests with those of the principal. Making subordinate pay depend on returns to the principal aligns the subordinate's optimal behavior with the principal's interests. For risk-neutral subordinates, the problem is trivial – one just rewards the subordinate based on the returns to the principal. With a risk-averse subordinate, the alignment of interest comes at a cost since an incentive based on the principal's returns will vary based on random environmental events. This means the risk-averse subordinate will incur risks so the principal must provide the subordinate with higher expected returns to compensate for such risk. Risk aversion in these theories is modeled as the rational reaction of a decision-maker with a risk-averse utility function.

Some agency arguments take a slightly different direction by arguing that principals can monitor subordinates if they have appropriate incentives to do so. In firms with widely dispersed stock, small stockholders have little incentive or ability to monitor management. This line of agency theory argues that institutional arrangements, such as outsiders on boards and having concentrated ownership (which gives the outsiders sufficient incentive and ability to control management), improve firm performance.

Several features of these models merit note. They assume the principal is trustworthy – top management's or the board's promises can be completely trusted.[11] They assume the objective is simple – maximizing shareholder wealth or monetary returns to the principal. They generally deal with only one principal and one subordinate; assume a very simple utility function for both principal and subordinate; ignore the possibility of time-scale issues where a subordinate may be able to look good on a given measure by activities that hurt other measures or future activities; and assume no complex interactions among multiple subordinates.

Agency theory's predictions come from the ad hoc assumptions of risk-neutral principals and risk-averse agents rather than fundamental tenets of utility theory. Excluding the incentive system, agency models assume that actions correlated with corporate performance reduce agent utility. Assuming that individuals get utility from working for a successful organization, or get utility from doing a good job (with good defined in conventional productive terms), would radically transform the agency problem. Indeed, the agency theory assumptions about human motivation look like the 1950s Theory X – a view that people are amoral and lazy and only work under duress or incentives. An immense literature on what actually motivates individuals clearly and strongly rejects these assumptions. While individuals certainly respond to incentives, empirical results clearly reject the assumptions of complete amorality and sloth.

The agency theory predictions depend critically on these clearly incorrect *ad hoc* assumptions. Studies that actually look at what motivates individuals show the limits of the agency assumptions (Kanfer, 1990; Pinder, 1984).

Agency theories in strategy make three basic predictions: incentives increase performance, controls increase performance, and incentives modify subordinates' risk-related choices. Most tests of agency theory examine the first two issues – do firms with stronger incentives for top management and/or stronger controls (e.g., outside board members, block stock ownership, etc.) do better than firms without? To hypothesize that controls and incentives increase performance requires assuming that most firms have insufficient controls and incentives. Scholars justify this by allusions to division of ownership, but an efficient market for corporate control should have solved this problem. If increasing incentives and controls generally increases firm performance, a profit opportunity exists where one could buy firms and improve their performance by increased controls and incentives (a rule for riches).

While the results have been mixed, many studies support the agency predictions. These studies often suffer from the endogeneity problem that the incentive or monitoring arrangements observed could be influenced by expectations about performance. For example, managers who anticipate their corporation will earn high profits should want incentive pay while those who anticipate low performance may avoid it. This could create an association between observed incentives and performance even if incentives did not change behavior.

Whereas serious study of agency issues started relatively recently, organizations theorists have been dealing with motivation for many decades (see Pinder (1984) or Kanfer (1990) for an introduction). The long history of organizations work has allowed the field to go in several directions. I will attempt to summarize some of what I see as relevant to strategic management. I offer my apologies to my organizational colleagues for my poor review.

A variety of different factors motivate individuals, and the factors vary across individuals. While direct incentives strongly influence behavior, other factors do as well. Norms or morals influence behavior – I refrain from behaviors that might be in my interest because I see them as inappropriate (even if I'm sure I won't be caught). Social interactions matter. I may do or not do things either because they affect others I care about, or because others may evaluate these behaviors negatively. People want approval of their peers. People care about many features of their work – prestige, socializing with co-workers, self-efficacy (perceiving an ability to influence outcomes), being treated with respect, perceiving the work is meaningful, etc.

An active area in organizations studies deals with organizational citizenship behaviors. These studies examine employee behaviors that aid the organization but are not a required part of the employee's job. All organizations have such behaviors and need them to operate effectively. Identification with the organization and job satisfaction strongly influence such behaviors.

Oddly, academics who hold that incentives are all that matter work in institutions that could not function without many behaviors that are clearly driven by social norms (see the discussion of academics in the previous section).[12]

Organizations can have motivated employees without formal monetary incentives. Few good scholars are primarily motivated by monetary incentives. Alternatively, consider the US Marines. At the lower levels, officers and enlisted personnel face a very strong culture and strong norms, but almost no direct incentives – pay is standardized by rank and time, and promotion by standard rules. Yet, few organizations command the effort and loyalty the Marines do.

Because organization scholars have emphasized operational rather than top management employees, most of their work on incentives has not been directly applied to top management. Organizational behaviorists agree with agency theorists that incentives should increase reported performance.

Where agency and organizations studies differ on incentives is that the organizational folks address the unintended impacts of incentives. The general rule might be summed up as, "incentives work too well."

Any formal incentive system measures certain things and does not measure others. This pushes individuals to focus on the measured portions of the job and ignore other activities. In corporations, incentives for departmental performance discourage departments from helping other departments. Measuring individual employee productivity provides an incentive for employees not to help other employees. Grading performance on an absolute scale does not solve the problem since helping others takes resources. Employees also can expect that management will adjust next year's targets to reflect everyone's performance this year. Individual incentives reduce cooperation.

Furthermore, incentives encourage individuals to manipulate the measures. Individuals play to the numbers. Using standardized tests to evaluate schools or instructors encourages instructors to teach to the test. For employees, incentives result in efforts to play the numbers – booking non-existent sales, deferring sales if one has passed current targets, sandbagging forecasts to keep targets low, etc. We see it in corporations where manipulating earnings may be much more efficacious than trying to actually improve the basic operations of business. Corporate manipulation of financial reporting has caused massive problems and many bankruptcies in recent years.

Before leaving agency theory, I should note a logical implication of agency theory. Like any model that assumes rationality, agency theory assumes the agents know the right thing to do – they know how to maximize returns. This makes studying conventional strategy issues irrelevant. If you really believe agency theory, the only important issue is how to get the subordinates to do the right thing. This may seem like a caricature, but it is not. This is exactly the approach offered in Jensen's (1998) *Foundations of Organizational Strategy*.

To summarize, both organizational and agency approaches agree incentives matter. Organizational work, with its closer empirical work, has highlighted a number of situations where incentives generate undesirable side effects. Organizational work also has highlighted other factors that motivate individuals. Strategy scholarship would benefit by relaxation of the total self-interest assumption, addition of more complex models of motivation, and additional examination of unintended implications of incentives and monitoring.

Summary

Overall, this chapter has attempted to demonstrate that some major lines of research in strategic management fit closely with behavioral foundations, while others would benefit from a behavioral view. Next, we consider the methodological implications of accepting these conclusions.

Notes

1   Additional confusion may derive from Hannan and Freeman (1977) using the term equilibrium but not meaning Nash equilibrium. They analyze equilibria as essentially the end point of a selection process with inert actors. This differs radically from the Nash idea that actors can act but cannot make themselves better off.

2   This is analogous to the structure-conduct-performance paradigm in industrial organization economics which largely ignores conduct and ties structure to performance because it assumes firms make optimal decisions.

3   Barney attempts to avoid this problem by assuming all choices are equally good (rational), but that some firms have rare positive characteristics (resources) that others cannot copy. See the discussion below on the resource-based view.

4   A referee on a paper in which I made this statement claimed it could not be true. I checked my memory of the statement with Howard Thomas, who confirmed it.

5   See also Peteraf (1993).

6   A colleague of mine claimed he believed Barney's argument and so decided that, if the interesting things that explain a firm's performance are so idiosyncratic that the firm's managers cannot understand them, then there was no possibility of conventional research in strategic management. He quit doing strategic management research.

7   Think of this as a research problem. The model of what determines firm success is often exceedingly complex and the available data extremely limited (since we really want to understand the success of a single firm, not average success in an industry). Could a firm reliably estimate the influence of each factor on a competitor's success? If not, then how would it know what generates the positive returns of a successful competitor?

8   This may reflect the equilibrium assumption. Equilibrium means firms cannot do things to improve their position. If untransferred but profitably transferable resources exist, then by definition the market is not in equilibrium. However, this derives from the arbitrary equilibrium definition, not empirical facts about technology transfer or market processes.

9   If we measure competitive advantage by profits, then we may be unable to differentiate between the two constructs. If so, why have the competitive advantage construct?

10 For example, if I used performance data on 100 firms of which 20 have sustained competitive advantage, I could get highly significant results from a model that explained performance for the 80 firms without sustained competitive advantage and had zero explanation for the firms with sustained competitive advantage.

11 Assuming principals can be completely trusted but agents cannot be trusted whatsoever seems to reflect an ideological alignment with owners and top management. I know of no empirical data on the relative honesty of top management and lower-level employees.

12 It would be interesting to see whether departments that from a scholarly standpoint subscribe to the self-interest model of individuals do less organizational citizenship behaviors than departments that do not.

5 | Behavioral Methodology

Given this perspective on the theoretical foundations for strategic management, what kind of research should strategic management scholars do?

First, note that most of the predictions of conventional economic theorizing in strategy make sense in a behavioral framework. For example, Porter's argument that barriers to entry help protect high-profit market positions works just as well in a behavioral framework as in an optimizing framework. Some of the details may change: a behaviorist might add to Porter's list of potential barriers the possibility that outsiders do not observe the performance of the high market position or that outsiders lack the information to understand how insiders work whereas rationalists generally assume competitors have good information. However, few (or none) of the sensible predictions of economic analysis require optimization and so would convert directly into behavioral work.

Empirical work in strategy seldom if ever tests the optimization predictions of economic models. Researchers seldom test whether firms have the optimal amount of something; rather, they test whether having more of something is good or bad.[1] For example, they do not test if firms have created optimal barriers to entry; they test whether having barriers to entry associates with higher profitability. This shows optimization assumptions are unnecessary – if the clear implication of optimization is never tested, why assume it?

A behavioral perspective poses some discipline that the economic perspective avoids. If a behavioral research stream assumes managers know something and that they make a decision in a given way, the researchers should check whether managers really know such things and follow such processes. A behaviorist also must be clear about the underlying mechanisms by which the model operates.

Scholars studying human behavior should talk to the people who execute the behaviors of interest. If you want to understand mergers, you should talk to people who have been involved in mergers. While an individual's description and interpretation of an experience may differ from reality, it offers substantial insight. Scholars studying a human phenomenon without talking to someone who has experienced the phenomenon resemble virgins trying to understand sex by talking to virgins. Such scholars (and virgins) risk fundamentally misinterpreting the phenomena of interest. Reading memoirs by insiders or careful journalists offers a similar although not necessarily identical insight.

Without an in-depth understanding of the behavioral phenomena or the actual behaviors in the field to complement statistical analysis, a scholar risks grossly mis-specifying the causal model. The scholar may assume certain variables act in certain ways when other variables drive the decision, and the variables of interest simply correlate with them. Furthermore, talking to managers often offers new ways to frame the problem: how they actually frame it instead of how we imagine they frame it. If I want to know if my theory of how someone behaves is correct, my study should include asking the person.

Let me give a couple of examples. The capital investment literature in finance frames the investment problem as selecting among well-defined projects. The tools recommended ignore availability of funds because the theory assumes a firm with good projects can obtain financing. The tools say nothing about generating projects. Bower (1970) and Bromiley (1986) find managers face a different problem. Projects do not lie around with cashflow forecasts attached. Developing good projects poses the greatest challenge. Forecasts have very low reliability and managers modify forecasts for reasons unrelated to accurate prediction. The availability of funds influences managerial evaluations of projects.

Doing my dissertation on corporate capital investment, I read much of the economics literature on capital investment. In interviewing the comptroller of a Fortune 500 company, I asked whether they used internal rate of return, net present value, and so forth. After a short while he stopped me and said, "Kid, we're not half as sophisticated as you think we are." His company used a hurdle rate of undiscounted 25 percent return on investment over a five-year horizon. The company was quite busy with projects with such projected returns. If I had done a survey without interviewing the manager, I might have fundamentally misunderstood what was going on. Indeed, in my dissertation I found another company that did exactly the opposite of what all the literature said – it increased capital investment when sales were down rather than decreasing it – and they told me this. I did not believe them when they told me, but the quantitative accounting data supported their statements. Without interviewing this company, I would not have understood why they did this, what logic lay behind this particular activity.[2]

This leads to another empirical tradition that underlay early work in the Carnegie approach. Bromiley (1986) lays out the methodology that Simon (1997b) recommends. To use information-processing to understand a firm's behavior, a researcher can track the firm's relevant information flows, ask how people use the information, see how people frame their problems, and develop a description of the process. From this description, the researcher derives testable models. Thus, Bromiley (1986) describes the process of determining the level of capital expenditure in several corporations, develops models based on the description, and then tests those models (models specific to a given corporation) using quantitative data from historical records on the corporation. This methodology uses qualitative data to generate models of processes that can then be tested on quantitative data. Such testing can use quantitative data on the firms examined qualitatively (thus testing the correctness of the interpretation of those firms' qualitative data), or on other firms (where it tests the generality of the inferences from the qualitative data).

This approach complements continued work using our traditional cases, experiments, surveys, and large-scale statistical analyses. Cases offer detailed understandings of specific instances – they help us really understand what is going on. However, case studies generate theories rather than test them. Experiments let us examine processes with controls not available in the field, and examine some processes we cannot study rigorously in the field. However, the simplified world of the experiment and the different experiences of experimental subjects, rather than the actual decision-makers, limit the ability to generalize to the field. Medium-scale statistical analyses based on surveys and similar methods let us test mechanisms and theories reasonably directly, but often use data from limited populations, raising concerns about the ability to generalize. Finally, large-scale statistical analyses let us find small effects that we might miss in small samples, and give us confidence in the generality of our results. However, they often use proxies that relate only vaguely to the constructs of interest and seldom offer strong tests of the theoretical mechanisms of interest. Each approach has different strengths and weaknesses; each has something to offer.

I recommend some modest changes in methods. We need sufficient qualitative knowledge of our phenomena to assure we ask meaningful questions and offer sensible answers. We might do more experiments. We might also do more studies that systematically use internal interview and archival corporate data to generate models of firm behavior that we then test statistically on either internal numbers or other data. However, no matter which technique we use, we must try to test whether the mechanisms we hypothesize are those actually in operation. Just testing aggregate predictions is insufficient.

Scholars who know traditional process work may ask where simulations fit in this approach. Early work in organizational processes emphasized the ability of simulation models to closely mirror organizational processes. Thus, the Cyert and March (1963) report detailed simulations designed to closely reflect decision processes. It also reports an aggregate simulation (the duopoly model) of two firms competing in a market.

Process scholars have applied simulation in two different ways. Early work attempted to develop complex simulations that closely mimicked actual organizational processes (cf. Crecine, 1967, 1969). This paralleled a general movement at that time to building complex simulation models of various systems (see Naylor (1979) and Rosenkranz (1979) for corporate strategy simulations). Simulation had freed scholars from technical constraints on complexity so they built models that relatively closely matched the perceived reality.

Over time, complex organization-specific simulations have become less common. Their complexity makes such simulations hard to understand. Being organization-specific and complex with many design choices, the simulations are hard to test. With the organization-specific detail, scholars have difficulty drawing general findings from such simulations. However, cognitive psychology's simulations of problem-solving face similar drawbacks and have had success by identifying a number of general constructs (production functions, search patterns, task environment representation) that apply to people solving a variety of problems. I do not know if strategy scholars could develop similar general constructs and use them productively.

Instead of complex organization-specific simulations, recent organizations and strategy researchers have used simulation to derive the implications of relatively simple models that may not have analytical solutions. Nelson and Winter (1982) model competitive interactions based on stochastic models of technological change. March (1999) reports numerous simulations dealing with issues such as local or global search and population change. Lant and Mezias (1990) simulate a learning and entrepreneurship model. Carroll and Harrison (1993, 1994) simulate a model of relative fitness and selection. The literature contains many other examples.

I suspect we will continue to use these simpler models more than complex simulations. Complex simulation models are hard to present and understand. I have found even simple models challenging to explain. In addition, simple simulations more easily tie back to specific general constructs than complex models.

Testing is also easier in simple simulations than complex, although I prefer econometric models to either. Testing the fit of a complex model to the organization on which it was created presents a very low hurdle since the model's many structural features have been tailored to that organization. The simpler the model, the more interesting such a test might be. Simulations that depend on few parameters can be tested on broader samples of firms by using parameters from firms to predict their outcomes. Bromiley (1986), for example, presents a simple, non-linear model of the determinants of capital investment. This could be represented in a simulation and used to predict investment for a large population of firms over time. However, many simulations do not lend themselves to such applications; the specifics of the models do not relate directly to observable field data.

Opinions about the relative advantages of an approach depend on predictions of costs and benefits. While some clever new applications of complex simulations might demonstrate unexpected value, I see simulations as largely letting us represent and derive the implications of models that lack analytical solutions. I prefer testing hypotheses from such simulations with statistical tools rather than trying to directly predict with the simulation. We have more experience with and tools for empirical testing in statistical than simulation frameworks.

The Importance of Process

This emphasis on understanding behavior qualitatively to generate more aggregate models comes back to the importance of understanding the process by which a theory works. When multiple theories make the same prediction on the aggregate data, we need process understandings and predictions to compare them.

Becker (1971) shows that the major implication of economic consumer behavior analysis comes not from assumptions about optimization but rather directly from assuming households face budget constraints. No finding about this implication can readily differentiate among models of consumer decision-making – almost any model with a budget constraint makes similar predictions, and the budget constraint is an ancillary assumption rather than a theoretical foundation.

Ancillary assumptions often relate our constructs to empirical measures. Consider strategy's uses of advertising-to-sales or R&D-to-sales ratios. Transaction cost economics studies use them to indicate specific assets for which contracts are difficult to write. RBV scholars have seen them as implying unobservable but important resources. Industrial organization scholars view them as barriers to entry. Some may see them as indicators of product differentiation and technology strategies. They also measure actual expenditures on sales and R&D – budgetary expenditures based on some internal management systems. Several theories predict a positive relation between these variables and performance. How can we differentiate among these theories?

If the theories made specific quantitative predictions about the relations, we could use aggregate estimates to differentiate among the theories, but few of our theories make quantitative predictions. Our theories say "a positive association," not "the coefficient should be 5."

Aggregate analysis cannot differentiate among these causal mechanisms. We need more micro-level empirical work to see which causal mechanism actually causes the aggregate relations (Bromiley, 1981). This creates problems for theories with unclear causal mechanisms. An advantage of a behavioral approach is that these micro-processes can be clearly identified based on direct examination of the phenomena being studied.

Simon believed in explaining phenomena by understanding the processes that generate the observed phenomena.[3] This emphasis goes back to "Proverbs of Administration" (Simon, 1946). At that time, scholars sought general rules such as "a manager should supervise seven employees" or "specialization increases efficiency." Simon (1946) argues that scholars should not search for such general rules of administration. The search for general rules leads to vacuous or contradictory principles. For example, proverbs often come in contradictory pairs – a stitch in time saves nine, but look before you leap.

Instead, Simon argued that scholars need to understand the processes by which organizations operate.[4] Such understanding requires knowing what decisions individuals make and the influences they face in making such decisions. This leads directly to studying information-processing in organizations. Prescriptively, he argued that tying such understanding to decision criteria and performance outcomes would indicate appropriate ways to organize. In short, we need to understand organizational information-processing to generate meaningful prescriptions.

Simon's Proverbs of Administration may have some implications for strategic management research. To some extent, we do search for simple rules. Is diversification good or bad? Firms should have resources. Such rules may be proverbs.

Such rules are probably too simple. Instead of seeking simple general rules, we should take Simon's advice and try to understand the *process* that

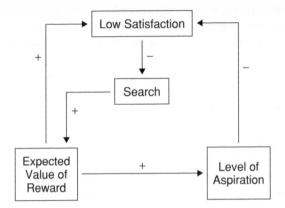

Figure 5.1 General model of adaptive motivated behavior
Source: March and Simon, 1958: figure 3.5.

generates the outcomes. If we understand how diversification creates value and how diversified corporations operate, then we could predict when diversification pays and when it does not.

Rejecting simple "proverb" rules does not constitute agreement with the "no rule for riches" position. Rather, Simon argued that a research program searching for simple rules would be unlikely to find useful prescriptions. Process understandings may offer more complex and contingent rules and understandings that may help the performance of many firms.

Organizations (March and Simon, 1958) offers a process understanding of how organizations function. It uses flow diagrams, a natural representation of processes. It emphasizes the interactions among individuals and the coordination of organizational behavior as foundations for understanding organizations. It presents process representations of relations.

Figure 5.1 clearly demonstrates this process representation. The *level of aspiration* and *expected rewards* influence the level of satisfaction. Low satisfaction results in search, which results in improved rewards. Expected rewards positively influence the level of aspiration.

This representation offers us several important methodological insights. First, we can see it is most natural to think of this representation as a dynamic model. Many of these things take time, so this calls for a time-series representation. Indeed, the text associated with this figure presents a time-based differential equation model for this system. Many areas of organizations scholarship are just learning the importance of time and dynamic understandings (see Goodman, Anacona, Lawrence, and Tushman, 2001; Zaheer, Albert, and Zaheer, 1999).

Second, this system can be examined in cross-sectional data. With "a few additional assumptions" (March and Simon, 1958), this model can be solved for mathematical equilibrium. Thus, if in a particular empirical exercise we know we are observing a cross-sectional process that has reached a stable state, a cross-sectional analysis could be productive.

Third, this process does not have to stabilize to equilibrium.

The information-processing approach has been extensively developed in cognitive psychology. In this work, scholars have built models that directly represent the information-processing of individuals solving problems. Such models even make the same mistakes that individuals do.

This information-processing approach to both individuals and organizations is an example of what Mohr (1982) refers to as a process rather than a cross-sectional model. Process models offer many advantages over cross-sectional models, but have some drawbacks.

Compare the kind of work and knowledge that the cognitive processing scholars generate to the equally fascinating work in behavioral decision theory (see, for instance, Yates, 1992). Most of behavioral decision theory ignores process and looks for patterns where individuals differ from rational (optimal) decision processes. Thus, behavioral decision theory consists largely of an inventory of heuristics or biases individuals display. These heuristics are exceedingly attractive because they lend themselves to experimentation and to generalization to other areas. For example, a large literature in corporate risk-taking and much of behavioral finance rely on the individual results of decision-making under uncertainty (see examples in Bromiley, Miller and Rau (2001) and Shefrin (2000)).

In contrast, cognitive processing work provides a deeper level of explanation, but less clear superficial predictions. We do not get simple hypotheses that apply to any decision-making-under-risk task. However, this does not mean the process does not lead to fundamental understandings, for example the bounds on information-processing say a lot about how display will influence decisions, the limits on how people can integrate information to make decisions, etc.

Perhaps most important, a process study of actual decisions tells us how individuals frame and solve problems. Often, the problems individuals want to solve differ from the ones scholars assume they should solve. For example, Crecine (1967, 1969) finds that government budgeters emphasized shoehorning desired expenditures into an allowable expenditure total that came from fiscal policy or revenue forecasts. Budgeting studies had ignored the expenditure total and instead explained government expenditures as responses to public demands for government services (represented by average income levels, demographics, etc.).

Process models also frequently make multiple predictions rather than simply predicting some final stage. Bromiley's (1986) model of capital investment predicts not only investment, but also numerous ancillary corporate plans. As noted earlier, process models and Gode and Sunder's (1993) zero intelligence traders predict trade prices leading to equilibrium in experimental markets. At the individual level, Gregg and Simon (1967) and Simon (1968) compare a process model of concept attainment learning to a stochastic theory. As Simon (1968) points out, not only can the stochastic model be derived deductively from the process model, the process model makes additional, testable predictions the stochastic model does not. Such additional predictions often make process models more easily falsifiable than other models.

Process models offer a clear approach to representing the mechanisms that explain a phenomenon, not just to predict aggregate correlations. A good explanation uses the correct mechanisms.

Process and Testing

This process emphasis has substantial implications for testing theories. Many of our conventional approaches to theory-testing largely ignore the internal mechanisms by which we claim our independent variables operate on our dependent variables.

Consider a conventional approach to testing a theory. We use the theory as a mechanism that relates a given set of exogenous factors to the outcomes of interest (see figure 5.2). Testing the predicted associations between independent variables and dependent variables cannot differentiate among alternative mechanisms or theories. In doing so, we do not test the theory completely.

For example, early work in top management teams argued that diversity in these teams resulted in better debate and higher firm performance. The mechanisms were information-processing patterns, but the independent

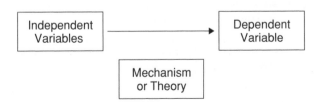

Figure 5.2 Independent variables, mechanisms, and outcomes

variables were team demographics. Finding team demographic diversity positively influences performance cannot in and of itself differentiate among alternative explanations. For example, does diversity positively influence performance because it creates more task conflict or because diverse teams have a greater breadth of information?

Our theories seldom identify a model without many additional restrictions (see Simon, 1997: 73). Utility theory is simply a statement that individuals behave consistently (Sen, 1970, 1977) – it only has empirical content when additional assumptions are added (e.g., that they seek wealth). An information-processing view says little unless we have some clear idea of the information being processed. Prospect theory says little unless we can identify people's reference points. A behavioral approach requires careful elicitation of the additional facts related to the mechanism, and, wherever possible, testing of the details of the mechanism.

Our theories lack the power to make predictions or produce testable models without ancillary assumptions (Simon, 1997). We use these assumptions to identify a model out of the general theory. Just as in econometrics, care must be taken to use factually correct assumptions – a model identified by factually incorrect assumptions is uninterruptible. We need to take care that the assumptions we use to identify the model from the theory are factually correct assumptions, and to test the most complete representation of the theory and its mechanisms possible.

Time Series and Endogeneity

Testing mechanisms and processes often leads scholars to time-series representations. Cross-sectional analyses represent snapshots or aggregations of behaviors that clearly change over time.

Suppose we have a factor X that varies across firms and influences firm performance in a population of firms. If X's full influence occurs instantly and it has no secondary effects, then a cross-sectional study may offer good estimates of X's influence.

However, most of our variables change over time and influence firms with lags. Assume for simplicity that the dependent variable for firm i in year t $(Y_{i,t})$ depends only on X_i n time periods before and e so $Y_{i,t} = \alpha X_{i,t-n} + e$. If all the firm X's have stopped moving and stayed constant longer than the time lag (n in the example), then β from the regression $Y_{i,t} = \beta X_{i,t} + e$ may be a reasonable estimate of α. In other words, cross-sectional analyses make a stability assumption – they assume all the outside influences have stopped changing and their impacts have worked through the system. This could be called an equilibrium but it is a very different equilibrium than a Nash equilibrium.

If, on the other hand, $Y_{i,t} = \alpha X_{i,t-n} + e$ and the $X_{i,t}$'s keep changing, then examining $Y_{i,t} = \beta X_{i,t} + e$ tells us nothing about α. Depending on α and how $X_{i,t}$ changes, we could find a positive association between $Y_{i,t}$ and $X_{i,t}$ when the relation between $Y_{i,t}$ and $X_{i,t-n}$ was negative. The model is grossly mis-specified and therefore uninterruptible.

A non-linear model compounds the problem. For example, if the model is linear and our observation period is long relative to the lags in the influence, then we may legitimately ignore the lags. Thus, if a factor took a week to fully influence a firm, in annual data we could largely ignore the lag and use averages. That is, the true model would be:

$$Y_{i,w} = \alpha X_{i,w-1} + e$$

And we estimate $Y^* = \delta X^* + e$

Where

$$Y^* = \sum_{w=1}^{52} Y_{i,w}$$

and

$$X^* = \sum_{w=1}^{52} X_{i,w}$$

Two of the terms in the sums would be mis-specified since the first $Y_{i,w}$ depends on an $X_{i,w}$ that was in the previous year and the last $X_{i,w}$ influences a $Y_{i,w}$ in the subsequent year. However, assuming those two weeks were not radically different than the other weeks, δ would be a reasonable estimate of α.

If the relation between Y and X were non-linear, then the aggregation would be suspect. Suppose, for instance, that Y was a function of X squared. The aggregate estimate would tell us little about the true parameter.

As in all statistical work, we need to ask how reasonable the assumptions are, not whether they are completely correct. No model can perfectly reflect reality – the more you really understand the phenomenon the more ways you know the model does not fit its intricacies. Which simplifications are acceptable is a judgment call that is strongly influenced by tradition, norms, available data, and available statistical techniques.

Nevertheless, many theories are naturally and appropriately represented in time-series models. Processes say factors at time t interact to create the situation at time t + 1. In recent years, substantial advances have been made and continue to be made in statistical packages to handle time-series and (even more common) pooled time-series cross-sectional data.

In all of these analyses, we need to be very careful about what is exogenous. Consider, for example, the diversification literature.

Traditional analyses of diversification used firm diversification levels to explain firm performance. If, however, firm performance influences firm changes in diversification (e.g., low performers diversify), then we might find a diversification–performance relation that reflected not a direct influence of diversification on performance but rather the influence of performance on diversification. Behavioral theories would predict that firms below their aspiration levels diversify more than firms near their aspiration levels.

March and Sutton (1997) make a general argument about endogeneity and performance. Empirical evidence strongly supports the behavioral theory's claim that firm performance influences firm behavior. This means that strategy scholars (who often study the impact of firm behavior on firm performance) must take great care to control for the possible reverse causal mechanism. The exact form of the control depends on the kind of model presented. The most common solutions involve well-chosen matched samples, appropriate controls in time series models, and simultaneous equation systems in cross-sectional models.

Notes

1   This creates problems since a rational theory would also need to justify why everyone does not do the optimal amount.
2   The company was in bulk chemicals. It invested when sales were down to have new, more efficient plants online when sales recovered.
3   This section draws from Bromiley (2004).
4   See Gregg and Simon (1967) for a similar argument on individual cognition.

6 | Where Do We Go From Here?

In many ways, this book is conservative, arguing that much of what has been and is done in strategic management makes sense from a behavioral standpoint. However, the real excitement is our future research. Chapter 4 suggested modifications and extensions of current research streams. Let me begin by briefly discussing some additional areas that deserve consideration.

Management Strategy and External Strategy

Traditionally, strategic management assumed that alignment (or interaction) of market and internal activities leads to performance. The argument for studying strategy as distinct from just economics and organizations rests on this assumption, yet we devote insufficient attention to its implications.

Most of the content literature and most of the process literature operates as if the interaction did not matter. We study diversification as relations among divisions' products and the number of divisions without asking how corporations manage those divisions. We study top management teams, but seldom tie them to industry environments or competitive strategies.

Some research has considered the interaction (see, for instance, Barr, 1998; Gupta and Govindarajan, 1984). Some process work finesses the problem by selecting a sample of firms facing the same competitive environment. But these are the exceptions.

If the internal operations broadly defined (which I will term management strategy) and the interactions with the environment (which I will term external strategy) interact in influencing performance, both management and external strategy research must adjust. Studies of external strategy that ignore management strategy and studies of management strategy that ignore external strategy *both* suffer from omitted variables problems.[1] For example, when we find that firms using external strategy X in condition Y have low performance, we cannot be sure whether the performance comes from the external strategy, or from firms using that external strategy employing an inappropriate management strategy. When we find that management strategy Z associates with performance, we cannot be sure whether management strategy Z is good or firms in desirable industries happen to use strategy Z.

Prescriptively, we need to understand how to adapt management strategy to match external strategy at the same time as we attempt to understand how to choose effective external strategies contingent on current management strategies.

This assumes external and management strategies interact in influencing performance. Several different situations might exist:

1 Effective management strategy might be independent of external strategy – the two are nearly decomposable (Simon and Ando, 1961). However, evidence in the literature suggests this is incorrect (see, for instance, Gupta and Govindarajan, 1984). Work and theorizing about dominant logic also rejects the independence of external and management realms.

2 Effective management and external strategies interact but firms know the appropriate interactions and optimally match management and external strategies. Bounded rationality makes this unlikely. If we do not know the correct matches between external and management strategies, why should we believe all the managers (who come to us to be taught about strategy) know them? How exactly would firms learn to match the two? Their observational fields are far more restricted than academics' fields, and suffer from all the same problems scholars know so well (non-independence of samples, sample selection biases, etc.).

3 Most likely, management and external strategies interact to influence performance. This ties back to the contingency literature in organizations theory, but also leads us forward to connecting deeper understandings of competition and management.

This interaction creates serious methodological problems. If choices of external and management strategy interact, then we need to consider both in our models to obtain consistent estimates of the impact of the strategies on performance.

Competition[2]

Our reliance on results from industrial organization economics and the historical emphasis on industry have handicapped our understanding of competition. While corporations compete in one sense, real competition occurs at much lower levels, at least at the business unit level, but more often well below that level. Airlines do not compete in air travel – they compete on specific routes between specific cities. All kinds of firms compete largely with those physically close to themselves. While obvious for restaurants, gas stations, and so forth, this is also true in many industrial products and services. Few firms have the same competitive position across the nation, but our analyses of corporate data often implicitly assume homogeneity across the nation.

For example, in aggregate studies of competition, Rumelt (1991), Brush, Bromiley, and Hendrickx (1999), and others find that business units influence performance more than industries. The industry estimate is interpreted as reflecting competition. The studies use national industry classifications. Any variation in competition below the national industry would appear as part of the business unit effects. This makes the business unit effects look larger and competition/industry effects smaller than they actually are.

We need to think about how firms actually compete. This would include:

1 Talking to managers about their competitive moves – let us make sure we do not grossly misunderstand our data. We need to understand how managers perceive and interpret competition. Let us also be open to possible explanations we did not conceive *a priori*.
2 Studying competition at the micro-level. This includes both the study of competitive moves along the lines of Chen and Hambrick (1995), Chen and MacMillan (1992), Chen, Smith, and Grimm (1992), and Grimm and Smith (1997), and more structural analyses such as the studies of New York hotels, including Baum (1995) and Baum and Mezias (1992).
3 Including behavioral models and understandings of firms and other participants. Customers, suppliers, government policy-makers, potential entrants, etc., all can be analyzed using behavioral assumptions. Porter (1980, 1985) informally uses behavioral concepts in his analysis, but this work can be extended and empirically buttressed.

Our emphasis on economics causes interesting blind spots. For example, the most basic economic analyses use the point where supply and demand curves cross to define price and so predict that a given good sells for a single price – the same thing should not sell for two different prices. This is called the Law of One Price. Think about the things consumers purchase. Few products in any supermarket sell at exactly the same price in all markets in town. The ones that do frequently have a monopoly position – for example magazines for which direct substitutes do not exist. Overall, the immense majority of products trade in markets with multiple prices. I do not know how this alters market functioning, but it merits consideration. Effective strategies in a world with one price may differ from those in a world with multiple prices.

A particularly interesting form of competition occurs when marginal cost is less than average cost. By marginal cost, I mean the variable costs directly associated with the sale of the marginal or additional unit. Simple micro-economic analyses assume marginal cost is above average cost. Economic analysis then argues that price equals marginal cost in a competitive market. However, marginal cost is very often below average cost.

Any time you have fixed costs, you risk marginal below average cost. In retailing, the marginal cost is simply the cost of the goods – all the other costs are fixed. Even if we count the labor involved in selling as part of the marginal cost (really a fixed cost with respect to selling the marginal unit), we still have all the other overhead and capital fixed costs. In selling manufactured goods, the cost of another unit is materials and direct labor, but average cost includes capital and indirect costs. In normal factory environments, substantial fixed costs in both capital and labor raise average cost above marginal for normal output volumes. In software and pharmaceuticals, marginal cost is very low despite massive fixed costs in development. In airlines, marginal cost is very small (an additional "snack" and a tiny amount of fuel), while fixed and average costs are large. A marginal cost below average costs may be the rule, not the exception.

A simple-minded approach to competition when marginal cost is below average cost leads to ruin. With market prices above marginal cost, a firm cuts prices, expecting that additional sales volume will increase operating profits. If competitors also cut prices and total industry volume remains reasonably stable, the industry finds itself selling the same amount as before but at lower prices. If marginal price is less than average, this process can lead to prices below average cost and negative profits.

The major airlines demonstrate this problem. Cutting prices to encourage customer purchases (because prices remain well above marginal cost) results in lower prices for all, and an industry that earns overall negative profits. Even without the low-cost carriers, "ruinous competition" existed in the industry.

This resembles a multi-player, multi-period prisoner's dilemma. If the players cooperate, all do adequately. If one player cuts prices (and others do not) that player does well and others do poorly. If all players cut prices then all do poorly. Rational analyses of this problem generally predict non-cooperation. However, numerous behavioral factors have been shown to mitigate the dilemma and encourage cooperation (see Komorita and Parks (1996) or Schroeder (1995) for reviews).

Empirically, some industries have managed to restrain competition while others have been led to ruin. We might look to psychology for some suggestions for factors that mitigate competition. Direct qualitative data-collection comparing cooperating and non-cooperating industry managers might also help. We need to understand how these important competitive factors work.

Competition offers fascinating and exciting research challenges. We must avoid incorrect limiting assumptions (e.g., that all firms are homogenous in various ways) and get down and grapple with the way firms actually compete.

Prescription

Scholars who take their data analysis and the limitations of their data analysis seriously often have problems prescribing. The folks who are surest they know how things should be done often just have a theory, or a theory buttressed by unsystematic data. Few of our empirical results are strong enough to give great comfort to prescription.

Consider diversification. Consultants confidently sold several strong models of diversification to managers – BCG matrix, GE matrix, etc. Backed by good stories, they offered useful ways for management to see their businesses. I find the core logic in the models compelling – considering industry desirability and your strength in an industry make sense. How-ever, we had (and have) no strong evidence supporting their predictions, and later theories reject their assumptions. Prescription based on a model without strong empirical verification is an act of faith, not science.

Alternatively, a massive empirical diversification literature with some underlying theory finds patterns of diversification that on average associ-ate with levels of performance, but the variance around that "on average" is quite large. Some related business firms do poorly and some highly diver-sified firms do well.

These two examples have very different structures. The BCG matrix and similar tools start with a theory and draw conclusions from that theory for action. If the theory was well validated and the conclusions close to the validated parts of the theory, then this makes sense. However, important parts of the theory had not been tested. The empirical diversification literature has some theory but relies heavily on empirical results to identify patterns associated with performance. This also makes sense if we have strong and reliable patterns, but often we do not. In either case, I would like direct evidence that firms that follow the tool's recommendations prosper.

Ideally, the two would come together; we would find an empirically valid theory that explained how diversification interacted with other variables to influence performance. The model would explain a substantial portion of the variance in performance. We could use such a theory prescriptively.

If our models explain little of the variance, I am loath to push their results too far. Indeed, many of our variables should not explain too much. We know many factors influence performance. None of our studies include more than a smattering of the variables we think should influence performance.

Probably the best compromise is to search for solid empirical results backed by good theory and use those. Some of the corporate governance and TMT literature seems to offer solid results. Alternatively, incorporating both external and managerial strategies may give much stronger results to traditional content and process domains.

Statistics

The statistical sophistication of strategy research will continue to increase. While sometimes I doubt the sophistication is worth the cost, it will continue.

Any data analysis must have maintained assumptions. For example, to run a normal regression we must assume the parameters are stable across observations.[3] As econometric technique has become more sophisticated, the assumptions that we make have changed. Some of these reflect good justifications and many just reflect common practice.

While sophistication has increased, the most influential papers seldom are the most statistically sophisticated. Theoretical papers have won many of the Strategic Management Society awards for being influential. First papers in an area often use rudimentary tools that later scholars extend and replace with more sophisticated analyses.

I have previously discussed the problems of reverse causality or endogeneity. Those, along with a variety of other econometric problems, will continue to push the field to more statistically sophisticated analyses.

However, more important than sophisticated estimation is estimation of models that directly test causal mechanisms. Having a more precise estimate of the impact of marketing expenditures on performance does not help us figure out why marketing expenditures help performance – it does not differentiate among differing theories that make that prediction. Better estimates that do not directly address the causal mechanisms may offer little insight.

Furthermore, we should remain modest about our estimates. We estimate models because we are not sure we have the right model, but our estimators assume the model is correct. The estimates depend on somewhat arbitrary assumptions. Furthermore, for those who really understand the process, all models are mis-specified – they do not reflect the complexity of the real system. All of this suggests modesty about our results. It also suggests that we should favor results that are robust to our estimation assumptions – we should question results we can only find with a particularly sophisticated technique.

Behavioral Theory of the Firm

The behavioral theory of the firm (BTOF) needs a variety of extensions and developments. Many of the extensions are not of central concern to the strategic management community as a whole – those of us who work in that theory directly will continue to worry about its microstructure while others do not need to do so. Partially for this reason, I have not included a section reviewing progress in the BTOF over the years. Greve (2003) reviews a portion of the literature on models of performance feedback, but substantial theoretical and empirical literatures address a number of other factors. However, some extensions may be particularly important for the strategy research community as a whole.

We need to extend Nelson and Winter's (1982) industry modeling of technological competition to other interesting domains. Nelson and Winter explain competitive outcomes using a simplified model consistent with the BTOF. They focus on technological change as a determinant of industry outcomes. However, a lot of competition does not hinge on technological change.

Using an evolutionary framework, we can build models to address numerous interesting strategic phenomena. Carroll and Harrison (1994) look at how firms of different types might come to dominate an industry. Other models could address almost any topic in industry analysis – a behavioral scholar could simply work through Porter (1980) and see how the results vary with differing behavioral assumptions.

Alternatively, behavioral work offers the most natural framework for considering learning and knowledge in firms. While rational models can deal with some very narrow forms of learning (largely forms of statistical inference from data), BTOF models naturally model both abilities and changes in abilities. Behavioral work also taps into massive literatures in education, psychology, and other fields on learning – strategic management does not have to reinvent learning. While "organizational learning" differs from individual learning (the focus in many other areas), we can certainly benefit from the individual literatures.

I am not sure whether the aggregate knowledge and learning strategic management scholars want to address is amenable to rigorous study. In the 1970s, organizations theory scholars devoted substantial effort to studying "organizational effectiveness." This effort floundered because organization theorists could not find generally valid measures of effectiveness. They sought effectiveness measures that could be applied to many kinds of organizations. Without good measures of effectiveness, studying effectiveness was problematic.[4]

Some work on learning deals with straightforward measurable issues such as production costs and learning curves (Argote, 1999). Analogous work in mergers may show that firms which do more mergers do them better. However, really identifying the learning in such a study is problematic – do firms learn and improve their selection of targets, their ability to integrate acquisitions, or do they simply raise their return-on-investment hurdle? Each of the three reflects very different learning.

I worry we will be unable to find measures of learning for most areas of strategic management and unable to differentiate between learning and other kinds of changes. For example, aggregate changes in labor productivity or gross profit margins could reflect learning but they could also reflect changes in management's emphasis on cost reduction (firing people does not necessarily constitute learning), capital investment (which sometimes reflects learning but sometimes does not), or even pricing (lowered wage rates or higher sales prices). If we measure learning by performance measures, we cannot differentiate between learning and performance.

Alternatively, training and R&D expenditures constitute the inputs to learning, not its outputs. Using inputs to measure learning assumes all firms and parts of firms use the inputs roughly equally well – a questionable assumption. It resembles deciding who won the race by who trained most, not who ran fastest.

The language used also frames the discussion in a particular way. Knowledge and learning both suggest the firm gets correct knowledge and comes to believe things that are true. However, top managers sometimes believe untrue things. Sometimes, erroneous beliefs can be widely shared across firms.[5] We must allow for the possibility of firms "learning" and "knowing" things that are incorrect.

Perhaps strategic learning research should focus on managerial beliefs and changes in managerial beliefs. Strategic learning should relate to changes in top management perceptions and beliefs. This ties back to the cognition and top management team studies described earlier. Defining learning by top management beliefs helps the measurement issue since we have tools for measuring beliefs. It also avoids assuming firms learn true things – we can measure changes in belief without taking a position on the correctness of the beliefs. We can also directly examine the correctness of changes in beliefs if we want (as the literature on accuracy of managerial perceptions has done).

Concluding Remarks

Strategic management needs to adopt a behavioral perspective rather than assuming rationality and equilibrium. Studying differences in firm perform-ance is of questionable interest if we assume rationality or equilibrium. Rationality and equilibrium assume all firms make optimal choices, but what is strategy research about if firms do not make systematically better or worse choices?

Strategic management scholarship can openly and explicitly take a behavioral approach. This does not mean doing "behavioral" work per se, but rather adopting a set of behavioral underpinnings for theorizing. Instead of assuming a firm optimizes, scholars should assume most firms seek to improve profits. Empirically, this fits the facts. We seldom find evidence of firms optimizing, but we do find frequent evidence of seeking to improve profits.[6] Pragmatically, it justifies many of the same predictions as optimizing assumptions while avoiding the traps and logical inconsist-encies that optimization assumptions create.

Taking such a perspective allows increased communication and exchange among the different areas of strategic management scholarship. For ex-ample, we cannot explain acquisition decisions as efforts for positive returns made with reasonable forecasts. Interchange among the cognitive, top management team, and acquisitions communities may offer insights. The cognitive and top management team literatures deal extensively with potential explanations for biased expectations and differing qualities of decision-making while the acquisitions community has a deep understand-ing of the phenomenon. Without being overly optimistic, it opens the possibility of collaboration between the previously disjointed areas of strategy scholarship.

A behavioral view also helps our understanding of competition. In many areas, we see substantial diversity. Restaurants vary from massive organizations like McDonald's down to family-run businesses with a half-dozen tables. Consulting varies from immense global organizations to solo practitioners. Conventional economic models of competition with minimum efficient scale, equilibrium, etc., are hard pressed to allow, let alone explain, such diversity. We need behavioral models that accommodate such diversity and complexity.

Finally, we need to test the causal connections and mechanisms of our theories as directly as possible. Only through the mechanisms can we differentiate alternative reasonable explanations, and really test our theories.

The approach presented here supports much of what has gone on in strategic management research. We should move forward unapologetically, using a behavioral theoretical foundation.

Notes

1 In general, if the true model includes a variable that is omitted from the model estimated and that omitted variable correlates with any of the included variables, the parameter estimates are biased and inconsistent.

2 This section draws on Bromiley, Papenhausen, and Borchert (2002).

3 There are random coefficient models that substitute different assumptions for the coefficients, but do not eliminate the need to make assumptions.

4 Strategy scholars deal with a research agenda very similar to organizational effectiveness but our focus on for-profit firms lets us use profits and similar measures.

5 Erroneous beliefs can be easily identified in some major corporate errors. Coca-Cola obviously misestimated customer reaction to New Coke, and IBM misestimated reaction to the PC Junior. Widely shared erroneous beliefs may be harder to demonstrate. To offer a simple example, not that long ago many large corporations had policies based on erroneous beliefs about the abilities of women, minorities, age groups, etc.

6 Managers may use the term optimize when they really mean seek. Few would really claim to have optimized in the economist's terms of finding the best of all possible choices for all actions and processes in the firm. Differences in economic and managerial use of language should not be used to misconstrue what managers say.

References

Amburgey, T. L., Kelly, D. and Barnett, W. P. (1993) "Resetting the Clock: The Dynamics of Organizational Change and Failure," *Administrative Science Quarterly*, 38(1), 51–73.

Amburgey, T. L. and Miner, A. S. (1992) "Strategic Momentum: The Effects of Repetitive, Positional, and Contextual Momentum on Merger Activity," *Strategic Management Journal*, 13(5), 335–48.

Amihud, Y. and Lev, B. (1981) "Risk Reduction as a Managerial Motive for Conglomerate Mergers," *Bell Journal of Economics*, 12(2), 605–17.

Andrews, K. R. (1971) *The Concept of Corporate Strategy*, Homewood, IL: Richard D. Irwin.

Argote, L. (1999) *Organizational Learning: Creating, Retaining, and Transferring Knowledge*, Boston, MA: Kluwer Academic.

Argyris, C. (1973) "Some Limits of Rational Man Organizational Theory," *Public Administration Review*, 33(3), 253–67.

Argyris, C. (1976) "Single-Loop and Double-Loop Models in Research on Decision Making," *Administrative Science Quarterly*, 21(3), 363–75.

Armour, H. O. and Teece, D. J. (1978) "Organizational Structure and Economic Performance: A Test of the Multidivisional Hypothesis," *Bell Journal of Economics*, 9(1), 106–22.

Arrow, K. J. (1986) "Rationality of Self and Others in an Economic System," *Journal of Business*, 59(4), S385–S399.

Arrow, K. J. (2004) "Is Bounded Rationality Unboundedly Rational? Some Ruminations," in M. Augier and J. G. March (eds), *Essays in Honor of Herbert Simon*, pp. 47–56, Cambridge, MA: MIT Press.

Barnes, R. and Sheppard, E. (1992) "Is There a Place for the Rational Actor? A Geographical Critique of the Rational Choice Paradigm," *Economic Geography*, 68, 1–21.

Barney, J. B. (1986) "Strategic Factor Markets: Expectations, Luck, and Business Strategy," *Management Science*, 32, 1231–41.

Barney, J. B. (1991) "Firm Resources and Sustained Competitive Advantage," *Journal of Management*, 17, 99–120.

Barney, J. B. (2001) "Is the Resource-Based 'View' a Useful Perspective for Strategic Management Research? Yes," *Academy of Management Review*, 26(1), 41–57.

Barr, P. (1998) "Adapting to Unfamiliar Environmental Events: A Look at the Evaluation of Interpretation and its Role in Strategic Change," *Organization Science* 9(6), 644–69.

Barr, P., Stimpert, J. L. and Huff, A. S. (1992) "Cognitive Change, Strategic Action, and Organizational Renewal," *Strategic Management Journal*, 13, 15–36.

Baum, J. A. C. (1995) "The Changing Basis of Competition in Organization Populations: The Manhattan Hotel Industry, 1898–1990," *Social Forces*, 74, 177–204.

Baum, J. A. C. and Mezias, Stephen J. (1992) "Localized Competition and Organizational Failure in the Manhattan Hotel Industry, 1898–1990," *Administrative Science Quarterly*, 37, 580–605.

Baumol, W. J. (2004) "On Rational Satisficing," in M. Augier and J. G. March (eds), *Essays in Honor of Herbert Simon*, pp. 57–66, Cambridge, MA: MIT Press.

Becker, G. S. (1971) *Economic Theory*, New York: Alfred A. Knopf.

Bell, G. G. (1999) *The Influence of Geographic Location and Network Position on Innovation in the Canadian Mutual Fund Industry*, Ph.D. dissertation, University of Minnesota.

Bell, G. G. and Zaheer, A. (2001) "Instrumental But Not Enough: The Influence of Individual and Organizational Networks on Communication Flows," paper presented at the 2001 Academy of Management Meetings, Washington, DC.

Berndt, E. R. (1976) "Reconciling Alternative Estimates of the Elasticity of Substitution," *The Review of Economics and Statistics*, 58(1) 59–68.

Biddle, Gary C., Bowen, Robert M. and Wallace, James S. (1997) "Does EVA Beat Earnings? Evidence on Associations with Stock Returns and Firm Values," *Journal of Accounting & Economics*, 24(3), 301–36.

Boland, L. A. (1981) "On the Futility of Criticizing the Neoclassical Maximization Hypothesis," *American Economic Review*, 71(5), 1031–6.

Bourgeois, L. J. III and Eisenhardt, K. M. (1988) "Strategic Decision Processes in High Velocity Environments: Four Cases in the Microcomputer Industry," *Management Science*, 34(7), 816–35.

Bower, J. L. (1970) *Managing the Resource Allocation Process: A Study of Corporate Planning and Investment*, Cambridge, MA: Graduate School of Business Administration, Harvard University.

Bowie, N. E. (1999) *Business Ethics: A Kantian Perspective*, Malden, MA: Blackwell.

Bromiley, P. (1981) "Task Environments and Budgetary Decision-Making," *Academy of Management Review*, 6(2), 277–88.

Bromiley, P. (1986) *Corporate Capital Investment: A Behavioral Approach*, New York: Cambridge University Press.

Bromiley, P. (1987) "Do Forecasts Produced by Organizations Reflect Anchoring and Adjustment?" *Journal of Forecasting*, 6(3), 201–10.

Bromiley, P. (2004) "A Focus on Process: Part of Herbert Simon's Legacy," in M. Augier and J. G. March (eds), *Essays in Honor of Herbert Simon*, pp. 183–90, Cambridge, MA: MIT Press.

Bromiley, P. and Cummings, L. L. (1995) "Organizations with Trust: A Theoretical Perspective," in R. Bies, R. Lewicki and B. Sheppard (eds), *Research in Negotiation in Organizations*, vol. 5, pp. 219–47, Greenwich, CT: JAI Press.

Bromiley, P. and Fleming, L. (2002) "The Resource-Based View of Strategy: A Behaviorist's Critique," in M. Augier and J. G. March (eds), *The Economics of Choice, Change, and Organizations: Essays in Memory of Richard M. Cyert*, Cheltenham, UK: Edward Elgar Publishing.

Bromiley, P., Miller, K. D. and Rau, D. (2001) "Risk in Strategic Management Research," in M. A. Hitt, R. E. Freeman and J. S. Harrison (eds), *Handbook of Strategic Management*, pp. 259–88, Malden, MA: Blackwell.

Bromiley, P. and Papenhausen, C. (2003) "Assumptions of Rationality and Equilibrium in Strategy Research: The Limits of Traditional Economic Analysis," *Strategic Organization*, 1(4), 413–37.

Bromiley, P., Papenhausen, C. and Borchert, P. (2002) "Why Do Gas Prices Vary, or Towards Understanding the Micro-Structure of Competition," *Managerial Decision and Economics*, 23(4–5), 171–86.

Brush, T. H., Bromiley, P. and Hendrickx, M. (1999) "The Relative Influence of Industry, Corporation, and Business Unit on Performance: An Alternative Estimate," *Strategic Management Journal*, 20(6), 519–49.

Caldwell, Bruce (1984) *Appraisal and Criticism in Economics: A Book of Readings*, Boston, MA: Allen & Unwin.

Camerer, C. F. (1991) "Does Strategy Research Need Game Theory?" *Strategic Management Journal*, 12, 137–52.

Carlton, D. W. and Perloff, J. M. (1994) *Modern Industrial Organization*, Boston, MA: Addison-Wesley.

Carroll, G. R. and Harrison, J. R. (1993) "Evolution among Competing Organizational Forms," *World Futures: The Journal of General Evolution*, 36, 91–110.

Carroll, G. R. and Harrison, J. R. (1994) "On the Historical Efficiency of Competition between Organizational Populations," *The American Journal of Sociology*, 199(3), 720–49.

Chen, M. J. and Hambrick, D. (1995) "Speed, Stealth, and Selective Attack: How Small Firms Differ from Large Firms in Competitive Behavior," *Academy of Management Journal*, 38(2), 453–82.

Chen, M. J. and MacMillan, I. (1992) "Nonresponse and Delayed Response to Competitive Moves: The Roles of Competitor Dependence and Action Irreversibility," *Academy of Management Journal*, 35, 539–70.

Chen, M. J., Smith, K. G. and Grimm, C. M. (1992) "Action Characteristics as Predictors of Competitive Responses," *Management Science*, 38(3), 439–55.

Clapham, S. E. and Schwenk, C. R. (1991) "Self-Serving Attributions, Managerial Cognition, and Company Performance," *Strategic Management Journal*, 12, 219–29.

Cohen, M. D., March, J. G. and Olsen, J. P. (1972) "A Garbage Can Model of Organizational Choice," *Administrative Science Quarterly*, 17(1), 1–25.

Conlisk, J. (1996) "Why Bounded Rationality?" *Journal of Economic Literature*, 34, 669–700.

Crecine, J. P. (1967) "A Computer Simulation Model of Municipal Budgeting," *Management Science*, 13(11), 786–815.

Crecine, J. P. (1969) *Governmental Problem Solving: A Computer Simulation of Municipal Budgeting*, Chicago: Rand McNally.

Curley S. P. and Benson P. G. (1994) "Applying a Cognitive Perspective to Probability Construction," in G. Wright and P. Ayton (eds), *Subjective Probability*, pp. 185–209, Chichester, UK: John Wiley & Sons.

Curry, M. (1948) *Yacht Racing: The Aerodynamics of Sails and Racing Tactics*, 5th edn, New York: C. Scribner's Sons.

Cyert, R. M. and March, J. G. (1963) *A Behavioral Theory of the Firm*, Englewood Cliffs, NJ: Prentice-Hall.

Cyert, R. M. and March, J. G. (1992) *A Behavioral Theory of the Firm*, 2nd edn., Oxford: Blackwell.

Dawes, R. M. (1971) "A Case Study of Graduate Admissions: Applications of Three Principles of Human Decision Making," *American Psychologist*, 26, 180–8.

Dawes, R. M. (1979) "The Robust Beauty of Improper Linear Models in Decision Making," *American Psychologist*, 34(7), 571–82.

Dawes, R. M. (1994) *House of Cards: Psychology and Psychotherapy Built on Myth*, New York: Free Press.

Dawes, R. M. (2001) *Everyday Irrationality: How Pseudo-Scientists, Lunatics, and the Rest of us Systematically Fail to Think Rationally*, Boulder, CO: Westview Press.

Dierickx, I. and Cool, K. (1989) "Asset Stock Accumulation and Sustainability of Competitive Advantage," *Management Science*, 35, 1504–11.

Easton, P. D. (1985) "Accounting Earnings and Security Valuation: Empirical Evidence of the Fundamental Links," *Journal of Accounting Research*, 23(supplement), 54–77.

Eisenhardt, K. M. (1989) "Making Fast Strategic Decisions in High-Velocity Environments," *Academy of Management Journal*, 32(3), 543–76.

Elster, J. (1989) *Nuts and Bolts for Social Sciences*, Cambridge: Cambridge University Press.

Fama, E. F. and Miller, M. H. (1972) *The Theory of Finance*, Hinsdale, IL: Dryden Press.

Fiegenbaum, A. and Thomas, H. (1986) "Dynamic and Risk Measurement Perspectives on Bowman's Risk-Return Paradox for Strategic Management: An Empirical Study," *Strategic Management Journal*, 7, 395–407.

Fiegenbaum, A. and Thomas, H. (1988) "Attitudes Toward Risk and the Risk-Return Paradox: Prospect Theory Explanations," *Academy of Management Journal*, 31, 85–106.

Findlay, M. C. and Williams, E. E. (1979) "Owners' Surplus: The Marginal Efficiency of Capital and Market Equilibrium," *Journal of Business Finance and Accounting*, 6(1), 17–36.

Findlay, M. C. and Williams, E. E. (1980) "A Positivist Evaluation of the New Finance," *Financial Management*, Summer, 7–17.

Fisher, F. M. (1989) "Games Economists Play: A Noncooperative View," *The RAND Journal of Economics*, 20(1), 113–24.

Fleming, L. and Bromiley, P. (2002) "Swinging for the Fences: Aspirations, Performance, and Technological Breakthroughs," paper presented at the Strategic Management Society Meetings, Paris France, September.

Foss, N. (1997) "Resources and Strategy: Problems, Open Issues, and Ways Ahead," in N. Foss (ed.), *Resources, Firms, and Strategies: A Reader in the Resource-Based Perspective*, Oxford: Oxford University Press.

Foss, N. (2003) "Bounded Rationality in the Economics of Organization: 'Much cited and little used'," *Journal of Economic Psychology*, 24(2), 245–64.

Fredrickson, J. W. (1984) "The Comprehensives of Strategic Decision Processes: Extension, Observations, Future Directions," *Academy of Management Journal*, 27, 445–66.

Fredrickson, J. W. and Iaquinto, A. L. (1989) "Inertia and Creeping Rationality in Strategic Decision Processes," *Academy of Management Journal*, 32, 516–42.

Friedman, M. (1953) "The Methodology of Positive Economics," in *Essays in Positive Economics*, pp. 3–43, Chicago: University of Chicago Press.

Funk and Wagnalls (1963) *Standard College Dictionary*, Canadian edn, Toronto: Longman Canada Limited.

Gode, D. K. and Sunder, S. (1993) "Allocative Efficiency of Markets with Zero Intelligence Traders: Market as a Partial Substitute for Individual Rationality," *The Journal of Political Economy*, 101(1), 119–37.

Goldberger, A. S. (1989) "Economic and Mechanical Models of Intergenerational Transmission," *American Economic Review*, 79(3), 504–13.

Goodman, P. S., Anacona, D. G., Lawrence, B. S. and Tushman, M. L. (2001) "Special Topic Forum on Time and Organizational Research, Introduction," *Academy of Management Review*, 26(4), 507–12.

Gregg, L. W. and Simon, H. A. (1967) "Process Models and Stochastic Theories of Simple Concept Formation," *Journal of Mathematical Psychology*, 4, 246–76.

Greve, H. (1998) "Performance, Aspirations, and Risky Organizational Change," *Administrative Science Quarterly*, 44, 58–86.

Greve, H. (2003) *Organizational Learning from Performance Feedback: A Behavioral Perspective on Innovation and Change*, Cambridge, MA: Cambridge University Press.

Grimm, Curtis M. and Smith, Ken G. (1997) *Strategy as Action: Industry Rivalry and Coordination*, St. Paul, MN: West Publishing.

Gupta, A. K. and Govindarajan, V (1984) "Business Unit Strategy, Managerial Characteristics, and Business Unit Effectiveness at Strategy Implementation," *The Academy of Management Journal*, 27(1), 25–41.

Hannan, M. T. and Freeman, J. (1977) "The Population Ecology of Organizations," *The American Journal of Sociology*, 82(5), 929–64.

Hannan, M. T. and Freeman, J. (1984) "Structural Inertia and Organizational Change," *American Sociological Review*, 49(2), 149–64.

Harlé, P. (1961) *The Glénans Sailing Manual*, New York: Adlard Coles Ltd and John de Graff Inc.

Hartwig, F. (1979) *Exploratory Data Analysis*, Beverley Hills, CA: Sage Publications.

Harwitz, M. (1998) "A Comment on the Significance of 'Profit-Rate Maximization in Interdependent Markets'," *Journal of Regional Science*, 38(4), 669–73.

Hayward, M. L. A. and Hambrick, D. C. (1997) "Explaining the Premiums Paid for Large Acquisitions: Evidence of CEO Hubris," *Administrative Science Quarterly*, 42(1), 103–27.

Hedström, P. and Swedberg, R. (1998) "Social Mechanisms: An Introductory Essay," in Peter Hedström and Richard Swedberg (eds), *Social Mechanisms: An Analytical Approach to Social Theory*, New York: Cambridge University Press.

Heiner, R. A. (1983) "The Origin of Predictable Behavior," *The American Economic Review*, 73(4), 560–95.

Helfat, C. (2003) *SMS Blackwell Handbook of Organizational Capabilities*, Oxford: Blackwell.

Hirsch, P. M., Friedman, R. and Koza, M. P. (1990) "Collaboration or Paradigm Shift? Caveat Emptor and the Risk of Romance with Economic Models for Strategy and Policy Research," *Organization Science*, 1(1), 87–98.

Hitt, M. A., Ireland, R. D. and Harrison, J. S. (2001) "Mergers and Acquisitions: A Value Creating or Value Destroying Strategy?" in M. A. Hitt, R. E. Freeman, and J. S. Harrison (eds), *The Blackwell Handbook of Strategic Management*, Malden, MA: Blackwell.

Hollis, M. and Neil, E. J. (1975) *Rational Economic Man: A Philosophical Critique of Neo-Classical Economics*, London: Cambridge University Press.

Hutchison, T. (1960) *The Significance and Basic Postulates of Economic Theory*, 2nd edn, New York: Kelly.

Ijiri, Y. and Simon, H. A. (1977) *Skew Distributions and the Sizes of Business Firms*, Amsterdam: North Holland.

Jemison, D. B. and Sitkin, S. B. (1986) "Corporate Acquisitions: A Process Perspective," *Academy of Management Review*, 11, 145–63.

Jensen, M. C. (1998) *Foundations of Organizational Strategy*, Cambridge, MA: Harvard University Press.

Jensen, M. C. and Murphy, K. J. (1990) "Performance Pay and Top Management Incentives," *Journal of Political Economy*, 98(2), 225–64.

Kahneman, D. (1994) "New Challenges to the Rationality Assumption," *Journal of Institutional and Theoretical Economics*, 150(1), 18–36.

Kahneman, D., Slovic, P. and Tversky, A. (1982) *Judgment Under Uncertainty: Heuristics and Biases*, London: Cambridge University Press.

Kanfer, R. (1990) "Motivation Theory and Industrial Organizational Psychology," in M. D. Dunnette (ed.), *Handbook of Industrial and Organizational Psychology*, pp. 75–170, Palo Alto, CA: Consulting Psychologist Press.

Knight, R. H. (1954) "Science, Society, and the Modes of Law," in L. D. White (ed.), *The State of the Social Sciences*, pp. 9–28, Chicago: University of Chicago Press.

Knott, A. (2001) "The Dynamic Value of Hierarchy," *Management Science*, 47(3), 430–48.

Kogut, B. and Zander, U. (1996) "What Do Firms Do? Coordination, Identity, and Learning," *Organization Science*, 7(5), 502–18.

Komorita, S. S. and Parks, C. D. (1996) *Social Dilemmas*, Boulder, CO: Westview Press.

Kornai, J. (1971) *Anti-Equilibrium*, Amsterdam: North Holland.

Krugman, P. (1996) "What Economists Can Learn from Evolutionary Theorists: A Look at a Way to Get Beyond Traditional Profit-Maximization Theory into Something More Realistic," talk given to the European Association for Evolutionary Political Economy.

Lant, T. K. and Mezias, S. J. (1990) "Managing Discontinuous Change: A Simulation Study of Organizational Learning and Entrepreneurship," *Strategic Management Journal*, 11, 147–79.

Levinthal, D. A. (1995) "Strategic Management and the Exploration of Diversity," in C. A. Montgomery (ed.), *Resource-Based and Evolutionary Theories of the Firm*, pp. 19–42, Boston, MA: Kluwer.

Levinthal, D. A. (1997) "Adaptation on Rugged Landscapes," *Management Science* 43(7), 934–50.

Levinthal, D. A. (1999) "Landscape Design: Designing for Local Action in Complex Worlds," *Organization Science*, 10(3), 342–57.

Lippman, S. and Rumelt, R. (1982) "Uncertain Imitability: An Analysis of Interfirm Differences in Efficiency Under Competition," *Bell Journal of Economics*, 13, 418–38.

Lipsey, R. G. and Lancaster, K. (1956) "The General Theory of Second Best," *Review of Economic Studies*, 24(1), 11–32.

Lounamaa, P. H. and March, J. G. (1987) "Adaptive Coordination of a Learning Team," *Management Science*, 33, 107–23.

Lynn, L. H. (1982) *How Japan Innovates: A Comparison with the U.S. in the Case of Oxygen Steelmaking*, Boulder, CO: Westview Press.

March, J. G. (1994) *A Primer on Decision-Making: How Decisions Happen*, New York: Free Press.

March, J. G. (1996) "Learning to be Risk Averse," *Psychological Review*, 103, 309–19.

March, J. G. (1999) *The Pursuit of Organizational Intelligence*, Malden, MA: Blackwell.

March, J. G. and Olsen, J. P. (1979) *Ambiguity and Choice in Organizations*, Universitetsforlaget Bergen.

March, J. G. and Olsen, J. P. (1988) "The Uncertainty of the Past: Organizational Learning Under Ambiguity," in J. G. March (ed.), *Decisions and Organizations*, 334–58, Cambridge, MA: Blackwell.

March, J. G. and Olsen, J. P. (1989) *Rediscovering Institutions: The Organizational Basis of Politics*, New York: Free Press.

March, J. G. and Shapira, Z. (1987) "Managerial Perspectives on Risk and Risk Taking," *Management Science*, 33(11), 1404–18.

March, J. G. and Simon, H. A. (1958) *Organizations*, New York: Wiley.

March, J. G. and Sutton, R. I. (1997) "Organizational Performance as a Dependent Variable," *Organization Science*, 8(6), 698–706.

Marris, R. (1997) "Comments," in Herbert Simon (ed.), *An Empirically Based Micro-economics*, pp. 133–44, Cambridge: Cambridge University Press.

McKinsey Global Institute (1993) *Manufacturing Productivity*, Washington, DC: McKinsey & Co. Inc., Global Institute.

McNamara, G. and Bromiley, P. (1997) "Decision-Making in an Organizational Setting: Cognitive and Organizational Influences on Risk Assessment in Commercial Bank Lending," *Academy of Management Journal*, 40(5), 1063–88.

McNamara, G., Luce, R. and Tompson, G. (2002) "Examining the Effect of Complexity in Strategic Group Knowledge Structures on Firm Performance," *Strategic Management Journal*, 23, 153–70.

Meindl, J. R., Stubbart, C. and Porac, J. F. (1996) *Cognition Within and Between Organizations*, Thousand Oaks, CA: Sage.

Miller, G. A. (1956) "The Magical Number Seven, Plus or Minus Two: Some Limits on our Capacity for Processing Information," *Psychological Review*, 63(1), 81–97.

Miller, K. D. and Shapira, Z. (2003) "An Empirical Test of Heuristics and Biases Affecting Real Option Valuation," *Strategic Management Journal*, 25(3), 269–84.

Mohr, L. B. (1982) *Explaining Organizational Behavior*, San Francisco: Jossey-Bass.

Mosakowski, E. (1991) "Organizational Boundaries and Economic Performance: An Empirical Study of Entrepreneurial Computer Firms," *Strategic Management Journal*, 12(2), 115–33.

Mosakowski, E. (1998) "Managerial Prescriptions under the Resource-Based View of Strategy: The Example of Motivational Techniques," *Strategic Management Journal*, 19(12), 1169–82.

Mueller, D. C. (1977) "The Persistence of Profits above the Norm," *Economica*, 44, 369–80.

Musgrave, A. (1981) "'Unreal Assumptions' in Economic Theory: The F-twist Untwisted," *Kyklos*, 34, 377–87.

Nash, J. F. Jr. (1950) "Equilibrium Points in n-Person Games," *Proceedings of the National Academy Sciences of the United States of America*, 36(1), 48–9.

Naylor, T. H. (1979) *Corporate Strategic Planning Models*, Reading, MA: Addison Wesley.

Nelson, R. R. and Winter, S. G. (1982) *An Evolutionary Theory of Economic Change*, Cambridge, MA: Harvard University Press.

Newell, A. and Simon, H. A. (1956) "Models: Their Uses and Limitations," in L. D. White (ed.), *The State of the Social Sciences*, pp. 66–83, Chicago: University of Chicago Press.

North, D. C. (2001) "What We Know and Don't Know About Economic Development," the George Seltzer Distinguished Lecture, Industrial Relations Center, Carson School of Management, University of Minnesota.

Ocasio, W. (1997) "Towards an Attention-Based View of the Firm," *Strategic Management Journal*, 18, 187–206.

Peteraf, M. A. (1993) "The Cornerstones of Competitive Advantage: A Resource-Based View," *Strategic Management Journal*, 14, 179–88.

Pinder, C. (1984) *Work Motivation: Theory, Issues, and Applications*, Glenview, IL: Scott, Foresman.

Poppo, L. and Weigelt, K. (2000) "A Test of the Resource-Based Model Using Baseball Free Agents," *Journal of Economics and Management Strategy*, 9(4), 585–614.

Porter, M. E. (1980) *Competitive Strategy: Techniques for Analyzing Industries and Competitors*, New York: Free Press.

Porter, M. E. (1985) *Competitive Advantage: Creating and Sustaining Superior Performance*, New York: Free Press.

Priem, R. L. and Butler, J. E. (2001a) "Is the Resource-Based 'View' a Useful Perspective for Strategic Management Research?" *Academy of Management Review*, 26(1), 22–40.

Priem, R. L. and Butler, J. E. (2001b) "Tautology in the Resources-Based View and the Implications of Externally Determined Resource Value: Further Comments," *Academy of Management Review*, 26(1), 57–66.

Radner, R. (1996) "Bounded Rationality, Indeterminacy, and the Theory of the Firm," *The Economic Journal*, 1360–74.

Rau, D. (2001) *Knowing Who Knows What: The Effect of Transactive Memory on the Expertise, Diversity-Decision Quality Relationship in Managerial Teams*, Ph.D. dissertation, University of Minnesota, Carlson School of Management.

Reger, R. K. and Huff, A. S. (1993) "Strategic Groups: A Cognitive Perspective," *Strategic Management Journal*, 14(2), 103–24.

Roll, R. (1986) "The Hubris Hypothesis of Corporate Takeovers," *Journal of Business*, 59, 197–216.

Rosenkranz, F. (1979) *An Introduction to Corporate Modeling*, Durham, NC: Duke University Press.

Roy, R. K. (2001) *Design of Experiments Using the Taguchi Approach: 16 Steps to Product and Process Improvement*, New York: Wiley.

Rumelt, R. P. (1991) "How Much Does Industry Matter?" *Strategic Management Journal*, 12(3), 167–85.

Rumelt, R. P., Schendel, D. and Teece, D. J. (1991) "Strategic Management and Economics," *Strategic Management Journal*, 12, 5–29.

Saloner, G. (1991) "Modeling, Game Theory, and Strategic Management," *Strategic Management Journal*, 12, 119–36.

Sargent, R. J. (1993) *Bounded Rationality in Macroeconomics*, Oxford: Clarendon Press.

Savage, L. J. (1972) *The Foundations of Statistics*, 2nd edn, New York: Dover Publications.

Schroeder, D. A. (ed.) (1995) *Social Dilemmas*, Westport, CT: Praeger Press.

Schweiger, D. M., Sandberg, W. R. and Rechner, P. L. (1989) "Experiential Effects of Dialectical Inquiry, Devil's Advocacy, and Consensus Approaches to Strategic Decision Making," *Academy of Management Journal*, 32(4), 745–72.

Scott, W. R. (2001) *Institutions and Organizations*, 2nd edn, Thousand Oaks, CA: Sage Publications.

Sen, A. K. (1970) *Collective Choice and Social Welfare*, San Francisco: Holden-Day.

Sen, A. K. (1977) "Rational Fools: A Critique of the Behavioral Foundations of Economic Theory," *Philosophy and Public Affairs*, 6(4), 317–44.

Shapiro, C. (1989) "The Theory of Business Strategy," *The RAND Journal of Economics*, 20(1), 125–37.

Shefrin, H. (2000) *Beyond Greed and Fear: Understanding Behavioral Finance and the Psychology of Investing*, Cambridge, MA: Harvard Business School Press.

Sheppard, E., Haining, R. P. and Plummer, P. S. (1998) "Profit-Rate Maximization in Interdependent Markets: A Research Note," *Journal of Regional Science*, 38, 659–67.

Shiller, A. (2000) *Inefficient Markets: An Introduction to Behavioral Finance*, Oxford: Oxford University Press.

Shiller, R. J. (1986) "Comments on Miller and Kleidon," *Journal of Business*, 59(2/2), S501–S505.

Shiller, R. J. (2000) *Irrational Exuberance*, New York: Broadway Books.

Shleifer, A. (2000) *Inefficient Markets: An Introduction to Behavioral Finance*, New York: Oxford University Press.

Simon, H. A. (1946) "The Proverbs of Administration," *Public Administration Review*, 6, 53–67; repr. in J. M. Shafritz and A. C. Hyde (eds) (1978) *Classics of Public Administration*, Oak Park, IL: Moore Publishing.

Simon, H. A. (1968) "On Judging the Plausibility of Theories," in Van Roostelaar and Stall (eds), *Logic, Methodology and Philosophy of Science III*, Amsterdam: North Holland; repr. in H. A. Simon (1977) *Models of Discovery*, pp. 22–45, Boston, MA: D. Reidel.

Simon, H. A. (1974) "How Big Is a Chunk?" *Science*, 183, 482–8.

Simon, H. A. (1979a) "Rational Decision Making in Business Organizations" [the 1978 Nobel Memorial Prize in Economics Lecture], *American Economic Review*, 69, 493–513.

Simon, H. A. (1979b) "On Parsimonious Explanations of Production Relations," *The Scandinavian Journal of Economics*, 81, 459–74.

Simon, H. A. (1986) "Rationality in Psychology and Economics," *Journal of Business*, 59(4), S209–S224.

Simon, H. A. (1991) "Organizations and Markets," *Journal of Economic Perspectives*, 5(Spring), 25–44.

Simon, H. A. (1992) "What Is an 'Explanation' of Behavior?" *Psychological Science*, 2, 150–61.

Simon, H. A. (1997a[1947]) *Administrative Behavior*, 4th edn, New York: Free Press.

Simon, H. A. (1997b) *An Empirically Based Microeconomics*, New York: Cambridge University Press.

Simon, H. A. and Ando, A. (1961) "Aggregation of Variables in Dynamic Systems," *Econometrica*, 29(2) 111–38.

Simons, T., Pelled, L. H. and Smith, K. A. (1999) "Making Use of Difference: Diversity, Debate, and Decision Comprehensiveness in Top Management Teams," *Academy of Management Journal*, 42(6), 662–73.

Smith, G. F., Benson, P. G. and Curley, S. P. (1991) "Belief, Knowledge, and Uncertainty: A Cognitive Perspective on Subjective Probability," *Organizational Behavior and Human Decision Processes*, 48, 291–321.

Smith, K., Dickhaut, J., McCabe, J. and Pardo, J. V. (2002) "Neuronal Substrates for Choice Under Ambiguity, Risk, Gains, and Losses," *Management Science*, 48(6), 711–18.

Sterman, J. D. (1989) "Modeling Managerial Behavior: Misperceptions of Feedback in a Dynamic Decision Making Experiment," *Management Science*, 35(3), 321–39.

Sticker, H. (1945) *How to Calculate Quickly: Rapid Methods in Basic Mathematics*, New York: Dover Publications.

Summers, L. H. (1986) "Does the Stock Market Rationally Reflect Fundamental Values?" *The Journal of Finance*, 41(3), 591–601.

Sutcliffe, K. M. and Huber, G. P. (1998) "Firm and Industry as Determinants of Executive Perceptions of the Environment," *Strategic Management Journal*, 19(2), 793–807.

Szulanski, G. (2000) "The Process of Knowledge Transfer: A Diachronic Analysis of Stickiness," *Organizational Behavior & Human Decision Processes*, 82(1), 9–27.

Thaler, R. H. (1993) *Advances in Behavioral Finance*, New York: Russell Sage Foundation.

Tyler, T. R. (1999) "Why People Cooperate with Organizations: An Identity-Base Perspective," *Research in Organizational Behavior*, 21, 201–46. Greenwich, CT: JAI Press.

Veblen, T. (1908) "Professor Clark's Economics," *The Quarterly Journal of Economics*, 22(2), 147–95.

Viale, R. (1997) "Comments," in H. A. Simon (ed.), *An Empirically Based Microeconomics*, pp. 153–66, Cambridge: Cambridge University Press.

Von Neumann, J. and Morgenstern, O. (1944) *Theory of Games and Economic Behavior*, Princeton, NJ: Princeton University Press.

Wiggins, R. R. and Ruefli, T. W. (2002) "Sustained Competitive Advantage: Temporal Dynamics and the Incidence and Persistence of Superior Economic Performance," *Organization Science*, 13(1), 81–105.

Williamson, O. E. (1975) *Markets and Hierarchies: Analysis and Antitrust Implications*, New York: Free Press.

Williamson, O. E. (1985) *The Economic Institutions of Capitalism*, New York: Free Press.

Williamson, O. E. (1999) "Strategy Research: Governance and Competence Perspectives," *Strategic Management Journal*, 20(12), 1087–1108.

Wilson, M. and Daly, M. (forthcoming) "Do Pretty Women Inspire Men to Discount the Future?" *Proceedings: Biological Sciences*, The Royal Society.

Yates, F. (ed.) (1992) *Risk-Taking Behavior*, New York: Wiley.

Zaheer, A., McEvily, B. and Perrone, V. (1998) "Does Trust Matter? Exploring the Effects of Interorganizational and Interpersonal Trust on Performance," *Organization Science*, 9(2), 141–59.

Zaheer, A. and Venkatraman, N. (1995) "Relational Governance as an Inter-organizational Strategy: An Empirical Test of the Role of Trust in Economic Exchange," *Strategic Management Journal*, 16(5), 373–92.

Zaheer, S., Albert, S. and Zaheer, A. (1999) "Time Scales and Organizational Theory," *Academy of Management Review*, 24(4), 725–41.

Zaheer, S. and Zaheer, A. (1997) "Catching the Wave: Alertness, Responsiveness, and Market Influence in Global Electronic Networks," *Management Science*, 43(11), 1439–1509.

Zey, M. (1998) *Rational Choice Theory and Organizational Theory: A Critique*, Thousand Oaks, CA: Sage Publications.

Index